Dear Exile

Dear Exile

The True Story of Two Friends Separated

(for a Year) by an Ocean

Hilary Liftin
and
Kate Montgomery

Vintage Departures

Vintage Books

A Division of Random House, Inc.

New York

A VINTAGE DEPARTURES ORIGINAL, MAY 1999
FIRST EDITION

Grateful acknowledgment is made to the following for permission to reprint previously
published material:
Doug Dorph: Poem "Love" by Doug Dorph (originally published in *Mudfish*, #6, 1991).
Reprinted by permission of the author. *East African Educational Publishers Ltd.:* Poem
"The Beloved" by A. R. Cliff-Lubin from *Poems from East Africa,* edited by David Cook
and David Rubadiri (1971). Reprinted by permission of East African Educational Pub-
lishers Ltd., Nairobi, Kenya, and the editors. *Nation Newspapers Limited:* Two articles
"Dirty Kwale School Closed" and "Police Battle Rioting Students" by Nation corre-
spondents, copyright © Nation Newspapers Limited. Reprinted by permission of
Nation Newspapers Limited, P. O. Box 49010, Nairobi, Kenya.

Library of Congress Cataloging-in-Publication Data
Liftin, Hilary.
Dear exile : the true story of two friends separated (for a year) by an ocean / Hilary
Liftin and Kate Montgomery. — A Vintage departures original 1st ed.
p. cm. — (Vintage departures)
ISBN 0-375-70367-5
1. Ramisi (Kenya)—Social life and customs. 2. New York (N.Y.)—Social life and
customs. 3. Liftin, Hilary—Correspondence. 4. Montgomery, Kate—Correspon-
dence. 5. Peace Corps (U.S.)—Kenya—Ramisi. 6. Ramisi (Kenya)—Description
and travel.
I. Montgomery, Kate. II. Title.
DT434.R36L54 1999
967.62—dc21 98-47190
CIP

Book design by JoAnne Metsch

www.randomhouse.com/vintage

Printed in the United States of America
10 9 8 7 6 5 4 3 2 1

Dear Exile

Prologue

Kate and I go way back. When I was in the fourth grade I pretended to have a friend named Kate to make my then best friend jealous. During math I'd write letters to the imagined Kate telling her secrets Lisa didn't know. Eight years later, as if to prove my supernatural instinct, I got a letter from a real Kate. It was just before college, and all three of my future roommates had written to introduce themselves. I was too cool to write a letter. Kate's was the last to arrive. All I remember about her letter was that she informed us that she wasn't a kleptomaniac, didn't drool excessively, and wasn't a Republican. As soon as I read her letter I called Kate and explained that she and I should share a room.

Little did she know what sharing a room with me meant. Kate's blond hair belied her studious, ascetic sensibility. While I was actively celebrating release from an all-girls environment, Kate had actually communicated with boys before. This did not mean, however, that she wasn't supportive of my experimentation. I would regularly enter our room at three a.m., flick on the bare bulb that hung only inches above her bunk, and start telling her how Charles or some other heartbreaker had flirtatiously sprayed beer on my shoes. Or we'd have to take that hour to hyperanalyze what it meant when Sam wrote, "I feel like a thief when I'm with her, Hal," on the bathroom door. Kate insists that we bonded during these late-night sessions. I guess I believe her.

Years later some things hadn't changed. Coming home to my New York apartment one night, I found the following note on yellow sticky paper in very tiny handwriting:

Hilary,

Since I'd be your wife if you were male,
And since you've never eaten a grape;
Since you have a lust for life
And for men whose initials form rhyme schemes;
Since you don't much care for spittle
Being dabbed in your hair by blow-dried women
And since you don't believe Noguchi's sculpture
Was his contorted feminine side trying to get out;
Since you must sleep with two pillows
And since your table at the library says, "but I love him";
Since you had to kill that girl you baby-sat for
Because she wore navy and looked so innocent;
Since you can't like just one part of a love poem;
Since you claim that being happy is not an invitation to sing
And since you are short and fuzzy-headed,
And since I love you,

(And since you sort of said I could)
I took your new green dress.

Kate

I didn't really kill the girl. And I don't think I ever got the dress back. But we were too busy to worry about such details. We were older and had less time for each other. Still, when Kate wanted to marry Dave (who makes me believe in love and that people are born to be together and that there's hope for me and all the rest), it was me that they called on a Thursday to say, "We want to get married at City Hall tomorrow, and we want you to be our witness." I tried to persuade them to wait until Monday, which would have been much more convenient for me, but they won.

I was afraid that Kate would disappear into married life, and she actually did disappear, almost right away. Kate's always had a save-the-world impulse, so no one was surprised when the newlyweds joined the Peace Corps and went to Kenya. As part of saying goodbye Kate and I swore to write to each other, but what that would mean didn't really sink in.

Then Kate's letters started appearing in my mailbox, smelling like Africa. Every couple of weeks there would be a new one, handwritten of course, on crinkled airmail paper with multiple foreign stamps. I carried them around with me, reading parts out loud to anyone who would listen. Mine sped back to her, typed at high speed, laser-printed on heavy-stock company letterhead, weighed and paid in the office mailroom. Kate had to bike into the next town to pick up her mail. There was only one mailbox for the entire village. She could always sight my letters right away because the envelopes were bright white and they were addressed in my handwriting, which was smaller and more pointy than any on the local mail. We were both impressed with the speed and reliability of the international postal service. Only my birthday package to Kate was lost (and she still refuses to believe that I ever really sent it).

In compiling these letters for publication, we sorted through them, changed some names, and chose what best represented the correspondence that lasted over a year. The letters that follow are most of what we wrote, and all of what we felt.

—*Hilary Liftin*

Part One

October–December

Dear Hilary,

This morning as the sun rose David and I were waiting by the road for a lift to the Peace Corps training center. In the distance, and coming closer to us, was a man on a bicycle with what seemed to be a woolly lamb tied on its back fender. It was joggling in a very limp way, but I suggested hopefully to Dave that it might be just deeply asleep. Suddenly, the man stopped, got off the bike, walked around to the back where the lamb's head was flopping against the wheel, and twisted it until there was a loud cracking sound. Dave quietly noted that the lamb was probably no longer asleep, and I agreed. Then, the man got back onto the bike and rode slowly away. We frequently whisper to each other, as a reminder, "Kenya."

While we were walking today, seven giraffes and a herd of zebras ambled across our path acting completely unconcerned by the fact that they were not in a zoo. Near the training center is a huge, shining lake where flamingos and hippos mingle on the shores, and in the distance, under the fever trees and through the herds of various horned beasts, we can see volcanic mountains and grassy plains. Sunbeams come through the clouds like they do in religious paintings, and you can see for miles. When it's dark, on the other hand, you can't see anything—without electricity, darkness is a thing for us to contend with. The moon matters.

So, we're here, Hil. For the next three months we (and about twenty other Peace Corps teachers) will be in this town for training in Kiswahili and cultural studies, and then we'll move to various villages where people have requested high school teachers. For now, David and I are staying at the home of a large, welcoming Kikuyu woman. We're to call her Mama Kamau—her first son was Kamau, hence Mama of Kamau. She's married but lives alone because, apparently, her husband lives with another wife in Nairobi. If I understood her right, she said he brings her bananas on some Sundays.

On our first night with her, she graciously served a stew made of rancid goat meat. (Earlier in the day, I had been looking for a match and came across a slab of said meat in a drawer.) I got a stomachache from it, which wouldn't have been much of a problem, except that to go to the training center, we take a *matatu*. Taking a *matatu*, as we have just learned, means cramming ourselves into a rusty minitruck along with about seventy other people, their chickens, loads of pineapples, jerry cans of gasoline, or tied-on babies, and careening along at a million kilometers an hour on what still seems to us to be the wrong side of the road. (My first time in a *matatu*, I got wedged in so tightly I wasn't touching the floor. Now I know to squeeze in next to a Mama because we women stick together, and she will probably protect me from suffocation.) Anyway, the morning after I ate the nasty meat, I somehow got positioned with my rump only millimeters from a kind-looking old woman's face. Since farting is considered almost a sin here, especially in front of women and elders, I made some "very interesting faces" (as Dave put it) on the jolty twenty-minute ride to our stop. As you can see, at first we had a lot of fun with rancid meat jokes, but they weren't so funny when she served up the same stew the next night. And the next.

One Peace Corps woman has already decided to Early Terminate her volunteerhood (it's been five days). Getting dropped off at her homestay to find four staring children, no one who spoke English, a none-too-clean pit latrine, no electricity, and one bucketful of water for the week's bathing pushed her beyond her limits. She spent the night at the training center and was on a plane for home the next morning. No one is very surprised she left because she had even seemed a little freaked out by the food in an Italian restaurant during our training sessions in the States.

Mama Kamau invited us to her Catholic church Sunday morning—lots of drums and singing under the tin roof. The whole three-hour mass was in Kikuyu, so even the little Kiswahili we've learned so far helped us not at all. Someone put English Bibles in our laps so we could follow along. Do you think I'll find God in Kenya? The landscape we saw when we left the church was almost unbelievably beautiful, though at the same time one always seems to be walking through dung and breathing dust. I love it.

Don't you worry, I'm wearing my sunscreen all the time. (Although I think it's too late to save my skin.)

Love, love, love,
Kate

Hello Hilary,

Other people are getting lots of letters from *their* friends, small Hilary. Could it be that you, you, my fuzzy-headed companion in your wacky shoes, could it be that you are a Lesser Friend than they? I will imagine that it could not be so.

I want to tell you that there's a vicious cow living with us at Mama Kamau's, and he's taken a particular dislike to our dear David. The cow waits behind the *choo* (outhouse pit) and then comes storming out to wipe gooey, bigger-than-your-arm cow boogers on him and to violently head-butt him. Once, when Dave was laughing too hard and not taking the threat seriously, the cow actually stuck his head between Dave's legs and lifted him off the ground. It was better than a rodeo. Mama Kamau came running out of the house with a big stick, yelling *"N'gombe mbaya!"* (bad cow!) and whacking him harder than I've ever seen anyone whack anything. Now, she hands Dave the big stick whenever he goes outside—just in case. She told him in Kiswahili, "David, I would like you to beat the bad cow." Dave said the whole situation reminds him of Russell Denniger picking on him in the third grade.

I sort of like when I have to use the *choo* in the middle of the night. You might think it would be a drag, but I get out my kerosene lantern and go out under the African stars (we can see

Scorpio here!) and try not to trip over the goats. Then I have to gently move the sleeping twin lambs off the doorstep of the *choo* so I can go in and squat over the hole in the ground. I'm sure it'll get old, and of course it's unhealthy, but I still like it.

Today Dave and I walked the long way into town. We passed through forests of cacti, and I almost stepped on a wild gerbil as he popped out of his hole. Two men in white smocks and white turbans, one walking a bicycle and one pulling a mule, told us in Kiswahili that we were going the wrong way. They led us on a twisty route through people's gardens and past purple jacaranda trees and over hill and dale, all with a view of silver Lake Naivasha in the distance, into the ramshackle, dusty town. It's Sunday, so along the way we were hearing people sing and drum in church and Muslims getting called to prayer. I began to shake hands with one of the men to say thank you and farewell, but he only shook David's hand, explaining that he could not touch me. On the way back, a woman tending the corn in her *shamba* asked which tribe we were from. When I said American, she protested that we couldn't be from the same tribe because of our "different stripes"—Dave with dark hair and me with light. She added that it was okay, she was modern.

Mama Kamau is still, a month later, serving us generous portions of rancid stew, despite our repeated offers to cook. The pot on her fire is like one of those magic pots in the fairy tales that never empties no matter how much we eat (in hopes of never having it again). It's just always full of rotten goat meat. But eating it is, admittedly, better than eating brains out of a boiled sheep's skull by the fingersful as Mama Kamau did at her party last week. She offered us a little piece of roasted lung, but I ate some intestine instead because it looked more like hamburger. (Last week, when she left us to heat up our own stew on the fire, Dave covertly made me an avocado omelet with orange Fanta to drink, and it was the most delicious thing I'd ever eaten.)

From what we can gather in our painful Kiswahili, it seems that Mama Kamau's doctor told her that because she is so fat, she really should eat nothing but bananas. That was three years ago. She's pretty tired of bananas, as you might guess. Every night, she sits in front of the fire on her little stool and picks up her enormous plate of banana stew. Then the ritual begins. She sighs heavily and closes her eyes. She looks like she'd rather die than eat. She puts her hand on her chest and just sits for a minute, staring at the stew. Takes a bite. Waits, looks up to heaven, and sighs again. I might add that this "only banana stew" reminds me of the story of stone soup made from "only" a stone. We try to cheer her up afterwards by laughing and pointing with her at the fuzzy World Wrestling Federation transmission she has on her little car-battery-powered television. She chortles and chuckles at the men getting pounded and jumped on, and the three of us bond. It's really the best we can do since our Kiswahili is still pathetic, and it's not her first language either.

Time here is very strange. Since nothing is routine, I notice everything and days seem incredibly long. Also the fact that it's summer here and it's November makes it feel like time hasn't passed into winter yet. I'm beginning to feel generally disoriented. Often, when I'm hitching a ride in the back of a truck, children will drop everything to start chasing after me yelling, *"Mzungu, mzungu!"* They might mean a very derogatory "honky!" or simply "white person!" or even "wondrous person!" depending on how you choose to translate the word. Sometimes, it's embarrassing to be called that and to be such a spectacle all the time. Sometimes, it's funny that they want to see me so badly, and I want to smile and wave at the cute little girl chasing us in bare feet. Sometimes, though, the child will run so hard and so long, it feels like desperation—rich, white tourist, help me. Then it seems like she's running on her last hope, and my stomach drops. We're both studying Kiswahili intently because it seems like our only way to begin to understand what's happening around here.

A few things I need to know about you:

1. Have you started your new cyberjob?
2. What's going on with Josh "Do-Me-but-Don't-Do-Me" Stack?
3. Where do you live?
4. How much do you miss me?

I miss you a lot.
Kate

P.S. Hey Hil, Kate has hurried off on one of her urgent trips to the *choo*. She has soiled her shorts on no fewer than four separate occasions. At first it was funny, but now I think she just wants attention. I am ignoring her because I don't want to reinforce this kind of behavior. My bowels, on the other hand, are holding firm. I'm not bragging, it's just the truth.

Yours,
Dave

Dear Kate,

You mention things like fever trees casually. I have taken note of your rather pathetic plea for letters and can only suggest that you stop describing me as fuzzy, in which case I will put all the other friends of Peace Corps volunteers to shame.

Rotten meat or no, Kate, oh how you've escaped. Don't think you can get away with it. You've got it easy. Look at me. Who will I be now that I'm post-college, post–college boyfriend, post–first job, twenty-six years old, alone in the world, and in need of some income, some home, some company? How in heaven am I going to settle—whatever that is? I'm willing to devote my whole sympathy quotient to your gastronomic nightmares, I'm just asking that you understand that I'm making a life from scratch over here. It's no cakemix.

I have obeyed my runes and leapt empty-handed into the void. Much as I try to explain to myself that I am in transition and that everything's going to turn out just fine, I'm hardly the happy camper we remember. I'm living at my dad's now. My eyelid has had a twitch ever since I moved in here. It's a delicate, fluttering twitch that others don't seem to see, but to me it feels like there's a bird in my head, beating itself against the window of my eye. So right now I hardly recognize myself. I wake up in a strange apartment. I hide away my bed and all signs of me. I commute out of the city—away from all my friends and the places I know—to work in a sterile office at an ill-defined new job in a big, generic office building on a highway in Westchester. I'm just waiting: waiting to accumulate a foundation of knowledge that will get me the right job; waiting to find my own apartment so I can make noise and be a person; waiting to hail a cab and smile at the person getting out and see that stranger again and again.

Most of all right now, I can't wait to live alone. The finances of buying an apartment are impossible, but I'm willing to make adjustments. No long-distance service, for example, no food on weekdays, drugstore makeup, factory-second panty hose, found art. I can't wait to acquire "homeowner's insurance." I want to have my stereo going when I fall asleep. I want all the messages to be for me. I want to bring home strangers and store their body parts in my freezer. I want to polyurethane floors and leave the toilet seat up (Oh wait. I'm a girl.) and throw away all the plastic grocery bags which wouldn't even accumulate anyway since I don't shop. I want the shower to be a hundred percent available. I want to have parties and not clean up.

While I look for an apartment, everything I own is in storage. Of course I never thought it would take this long to land an apartment. When I packed up my belongings in August I was like, Wool? Who needs wool? Now I'm cold all the time and trying to look professional while layering like crazy. Also, my dad and Genevieve's loft was not designed around the concept of privacy. I know that no matter how good a guest one is, one's presence is eventually annoying. The only way I can imagine avoiding this is to try to make myself invisible. So I am rarely there, wake up when they do (it's hard not to), and leave as quickly as possible. I bring home flowers and groceries, and I've got all my friends calling an answering service. They didn't request any of this, but you can be sure I would never feel the need to be so cautious and polite and adult if I were staying with my mother.

I finally settled the lawsuit with my health club for ten thousand dollars, so I'll be wallpapering whatever apartment I find with ten-dollar bills. I'm not sure the scar on my brow is worth it. I kept saying to my lawyer, When the mirror fell on me it was like my own face attacked me. I told him it caused great psychological trauma. I explained to him that they should give me enough money so that I end up feeling happy that the mirror fell on me. That's what compensation for incompetence is about. My lawyer didn't seem very excited by any of it. But ten thousand dollars definitely puts a spring in my step. It also allows me to have some fun, for a change.

So I came back to your letters from my spontaneous jaunt across the United States of America. Imagine this: not until the day we went to pick up a friend's manual-transmission car did Josh Stack see fit to inform me that he'd never driven a stick shift before. And I'd definitely never driven a stick shift. Turned out Stack and I were both sort of passenger types who yearned to be driver types, so we were mutually encouraging and supportive the whole time, cheering each other on when shifting from first gear to second, and so on.

Have you ever walked around the Grand Canyon? Stack took issue with the Canyon Rules, which forbade us trying to make it down and back in one day because we might die. According to Stack, the rangers didn't want us to die because it might mean extra work for them. Anyone else might have been distracted from this paranoid hypothesis by, well, the Wonder of the World. Not Josh. Me, I found the canyon to be very big. When something's that big, it's hard to know if it's real. I read the brochure over and over again, trying to believe that where we were standing had once been sea level, but was forced to conclude that Josh was right, it was a scam. Seriously, the drive out of the canyon at dusk was more moving than the canyon itself. It was only then, in the so-called gloaming, that the awe settled. Stack couldn't stop applauding the sunset. I listened to him appreciate the sun, and the West, and our driving abilities, all the way from the Grand Canyon to Las Vegas, where we finally found a tape of *The Rocky Horror Picture Show,* the sound track of which we'd been singing since the Hoover Dam. America may not have elephants, but it has more slot machines than you know.

Stack, since you asked, is something of a tease, if sharing motel beds across the country can accurately measure any points of character. We crawl into these beds to spoon, and when we do that I get a little "why not?" quiver, and sometimes I know he's got a quiver of his own, but in the morning it feels like a not-unpleasant dream. Sleeping in hotel beds, dreaming that I have a real fellow and a real home. In daylight, we get along splendidly. But I'm not convinced that we should do whatever it might be that friends do to become lovers. Stack is mostly just a skirt chaser. He talks about wanting a girl, or girls, and snuggles up to cute hipsters at parties, but never really follows through. Also, he sort of acts like an overgrown kid, bounding around in his overalls, safety glasses, and Joker grin. Delia says we're Sam and Diane. Harry and Sally. It's funny, even my brother said that I should go out with Stack. In fact, almost everyone tells me to date Stack. Maybe it's because he is Mr. Charisma, or because we banter so enthusiastically, or because he's the only friend with whom I'm physically affectionate. Having a thing with him would be entertaining, but I think you'd nix it, because you wouldn't be able to imagine it growing up into something substantive. Why play with a Slinky when you can read a book?

I want to address the fact that I will write these letters to you alone. I fully expect Dave to read them, but I want you to feel like an individual, especially now that you're married and all. Dave is really only good for scatological updates anyway. And I love that cow story, but, Kate, I think you should know that it's hard for a cow to be a "he." And before you shat your shorts did you say to Dave, Will you still love me if I shit in my shorts? When are you done with training and where will you go from there?

I don't have the list of things you need to know, but haven't I covered everything? I think you asked where I'm living but now I've told you. Oh, and how much do I miss you? Let me count the ways: I miss you like the plague; I miss you because you understand everything I say and because for all I know when I say I see blue everyone else might see green but I'm pretty sure you see blue; I miss you because when you get back you're going to be really different and dirty; I miss you because you're not coming to my Christmas party; I miss you because you're speaking Kiswahili and I can't and I'm afraid you'll never come home; I miss you as often as I check my voice mail (which is like every minute); I miss you because I don't trust anyone else's sanity (except maybe my brother's); I miss you more than I miss all my stored belongings and with a force that is just a tiny bit less than my desire to find a lifetime companion; I miss you because the park is covered in snow and I haven't been there yet; I miss you because I think you love me unconditionally and I definitely do you. This turned into a love letter. Is that so wrong?

Goodbye, my dirty friend, goodbye,

H

Happy holidays Hilary!

First of all, it was not a pathetic plea for mail, thank you very much, it was an objective presentation of a few facts and figures regarding my correspondence intake in relation to those around me. If you are telling me these will be Pity Letters, you can send them elsewhere. (I'll just pretend I can read the newspaper.) I also want to say, on the record, that I don't think it's normal for a man and a woman who are not relatives and like each other very much to sleep cuddled up together without ever addressing the issue of sex. Conclusion: Stack's gay. Call me a cynic.

So, training's over! After repeated hints from Mama Kamau that the previous volunteer had given her an expensive goodbye gift, we got her a watch from Nairobi, where one can buy anything. We had some last rancid goat, some last chuckles together over Hulk Hogan, and said our *tutaonanans.* I have to say, my Kiswahili is somewhat impressive (to me anyway). Just show me some cattle to compliment or someone to greet, and I'm all over that. (On the other hand, I did call Dave *"maziwa"* (milk) instead of *"wazimu"* (crazy) when joking with a Mama on a *matatu* yesterday. And I told a man at market that I didn't want to buy anything I was "just swimming, thank you." Okay, so maybe I have a little bit of fine-tuning to do.) In my Final

Evaluation, by the way, my teacher told me I'm adjusting well to life here. What she doesn't know is that I didn't change clothes, do laundry, or eat much in the States either. In any case, now it's on to Real Life in Kenya, with Dave and me as the only *wazungu* around, yippee!

We're moving to Ramisi, a small village on the south coast. We're lucky because most people there use Kiswahili, or another very similar language, as their mother tongue—untrue everywhere else in Kenya. This means we have a prayer of understanding what is going on without having to ask people to switch from their tribal language to Kiswahili.

There are monkeys, mangoes, and some coconut palms in Ramisi. There's even a river where we joined some children in throwing rocks to antagonize the crocodiles (yes, from a safe distance). The village is on the compound of a broken-down old sugar plantation and factory. It's strewn with big, rusted freight cars and broken gears with tall grass growing around and through the parts. The people live in the rows of cement housing that the factory workers abandoned, and we will too. Many of the "houses" have caved-in roofs or walls, and because it's also very hot and dry, without much greenery, the whole place looks a little like a bombed-out, postwar town. It's not that kind of Hollywood poverty where people live close to the earth in a pure, religious-looking way. It's just ugly and depressing. We're planning on buying a filter since our water, which comes from a borehole behind the school, is brownish, oily, and has sediment floating in it.

What will be our house is currently occupied by a weird
Peace Corps volunteer. She has been cohabiting with bat and
rat shit, dead lizards, and fist-sized spiders with red legs.
However, the place has a toilet (although it doesn't flush), a
kitchen (that just means a room with a counter since we need
to bring in the water and cook over a fire), and a wash-yourself-
here room (an empty room with a drain in the floor). We might
also have occasional electricity for the socket in the living
room.

All we know about the secondary school is that there are
eight classes of about fifty boys and girls each. There are eleven
teachers, all Kenyan of course. Dave and I will join as the
school's only English teachers, and I'll get the form fours and
the form ones—the seniors and the freshmen. Dave gets the
rest. Because of the schedule here, that means Dave and I
will each teach twenty-eight hours a week—Peace Corps
recommends we teach no more than twenty (which is full-time
because of all the curriculum planning and paper marking), but
we're both eager, so we decided to go for it.

Did you have your holiday party? For our Christmas, we
came out here to the coast, near our future home, with two
other volunteers to explore. We spent the morning of the 25th
wading in the warm, sandy puddles of the Indian Ocean,
avoiding sea urchins. There were millions of little crabs on the
sand with one big red claw each. For a nearsighted person like
me, it was like walking in an enormous field of red dandelions.
We wandered back to the town for passion juice (which you

would love even though it is fruit and therefore a relative of a vegetable). When, out of nowhere, it started to pour, we sat on a stoop and watched the chickens run around in the rain. A man waiting under the same thatching was curious about us and invited us to visit his house. His village was at the end of a winding path through the palms. We came into a clearing where the red dirt was immaculately swept, the gardens looked healthy, and the mud walls of the huts looked strong and smooth. After we chatted for a while, he asked one of his sons to climb a very high palm and bring down some coconuts for us. Then he macheted the tops off, and we drank so much coconut water we thought we could never be thirsty again. Did you know young coconut meat is like custard? As we ate it with spoons made from the shell, Ali asked us if it wasn't our Christmas today? He said we, and all people, may have different skin and different names for God, but we are all of one blood, we are all brothers and sisters, and with these coconuts, he wished us Good Christmas. I wish the same to you, but without the coconuts.

Love,
Kate

P.S. We developed the enclosed pictures in Nairobi, and David says to tell you that Mama Kamau's cow is actually much bigger than she looks in the picture. My little matador.

Dear Kate, who is so far away,

My Christmas party wished you were there. My homemade
Pillsbury sugar cookies with frosting imitating Mondrian,
Pollock, and Magritte wished you were there. Stack, who blew
me off for baking said cookies and is only nominally forgiven,
wished you were there. The mistletoe wished you and Dave
were below it.

The fifty or so guests, who were well behaved in my
mother's apartment, and who included but were not limited to
my brother and Emily, Delia, Rory, Dave Schisgall, Amy, Greg,
Susan Choi, Sam (from work), Jon and the rest, wished you
were there. The night, which had an early Christmas glow, the
evening sun turning all the Upper West Side windows golden,
the night was thinking, now where has Kate got to? The spiced
brandy and the usual foodstuffs, but especially the broccoli,
were sorry you couldn't make it.

And I—as I turned in half circles and quarter circles,
receiving bottles and pouring wine and brewing brandy—even
though I knew you would have come as a favor to me, had fun
in spite of yourself, and left on the early side, I was sending you
a first-class psychic bundle of fresh-roasted chicken, peanut
butter cups and store-bought eggnog, which I hope arrived in

good condition. There wasn't much spare room for love in that bundle, so please find it here enclosed.

Merry Christmas,
Hilary, who wishes you'd been there

Part Two

January – May

Hello small Hil,

I have been repairing a mosquito net for you. It is very good
that you sent me a letter. It took a while for it to get here
because of my move to Ramisi. This business of having to
write letters to keep up friendships definitely separates the
wheat from the chaff. I've been getting few letters—you are
wheat. (That would be the good part?)

Oh, January 10th, you think, Kate and Dave have probably
started their teaching! And oh how we've started. Oh, how.
I am currently sitting in a virtually empty staff room in a
virtually empty school. Wind is blowing through the palm
trees. It's flapping the paper Dave has put over the screen to
keep off some of the sun. There is one other teacher sitting
in the room with us. He's resting back in his chair, looking
at the wall, occasionally brushing a fly away from his head.
David and I have been sitting in this staff room now for a
total of twenty-seven hours over the last three days. Waiting
for school to start. It hasn't yet, although we'd been told it
would start two days ago. We are sitting, looking at walls.
Sweating. Basically melting away. It's sooo hot here, Hilary. I
mean, HOT.

When we arrived yesterday, to see only lizards, and dust, and a man sitting on a log facing a bush, we were a bit surprised. After he finished praying, Mohammed told us he was a teacher too and that we were all three a bit early. Which we were. Oh yes, we were.

I think Dave and I really might go completely insane. I tell myself, "Be calm. Go with it." The meeting was supposed to be at 9:00. Now it's at 2:00. We sit. The wind blows. It's 3:30. No sign of the headmaster. We wait. It's hot. People say time is seen differently in Africa. This is what they mean. I tell myself to relax. We wait. No work. I count sheep. I count goats. I count chickens. Mohammed prays again. I envy his having religion. We wait. The first student arrives. I listen to his footsteps in the sand. He walks to the classroom to wait. Wind rustles palm leaves. There's silence. We wait. Mohammed and another teacher talk quietly for a second. I hear phrases in Kiswahili ending with "and the bird died." I feel deep envy of the bird. Heat. Flies. Silence. Another hour passes. Another teacher comes. We greet each other. He sits. The wind blows. Someone writes something on a scrap of paper. Time passes. I remember Sartre's play *No Exit*.

At 5:00 in the evening the headmaster (whose eyes are bloodshot and half-closed) says, for the second time, the only phrase he has uttered to us so far, "Whoze zees Mountegoomery?" And when I indicate myself, he again walks off. I never thought I would live to see the day when I would wish to God I knew how to crochet. The newest teacher to arrive, only two days and five hours late, is sitting at his desk gazing absently out the window whistling three notes over and over again. It's too hot to talk. Another teacher is playing with a screw on his desk, rolling it around and around and around. The men who guard the school arrive carrying bows and arrows and wearing green outfits like surgeons. What are they defending the school against? Baboons? Appendicitis? Word inches out that it looks like today there are not enough teachers to hold a meeting, we should come back tomorrow morning.

So here we are, the next day, having arrived at 7:45 as instructed. Now it's 10:30 and there's only one other teacher so far. Let me tell you how much David and I are sweating. The first four days here, we didn't pee at all because we sweated so much. We're sitting here in this staff room, waiting, and basically pissing out our faces. We brought a watch today, as Dave put it, "just for fun." You know how my dad always says, "ABAB"—Always Bring A Book? Well, here, my friend, it's ABAB, BABAC (that is, "Always Bring A Book, But in Africa, Bring A Couple"). I'm sure you can tell me what rhyme scheme that is. Dave just told me he has to pee really badly but he's not going to go because it gives him something to think about while we're sitting here. There are now five teachers and two students here. The headmaster has declared it "break time"! What? Are we going to take a break from our marathon of doing nothing by having a ten-minute work time? Maybe we'll all switch seats for ten minutes and stare at someone else's wall. Help!

—*K*

P.S. I am amazed that you're still looking for an apartment. How picky are you?

Dear Exile,

Guess what! I found an apartment. Don't jinx the deal by being
happy for me, but it's a cute little studio-made-into-a-one-
bedroom in Chelsea. It has a dishwasher and Jacuzzi jets in the
bathtub and pretty wood floors. The bedroom has glass brick
windows through to the living room, which save the bedroom
from being confused with a closet. There's a little kitchen with
a funky tile floor, and I plan to paint it very brightly. The whole
place has nice fixin's (as my brother the architect calls them),
and the building is kind of fancy, with a doorman and a
beautiful roof, and, most of all, it will be mine and I will be
alone and I am excited.

I do feel a little weird buying this apartment. Because it's such
a major investment, I'm forced to think in bigger terms than I
want or like to. I mean, when you buy a place you need to
think about how long, realistically, you're going to stay there. I
like to pretend that my future is up in the air, that I have no
idea what I want and that anything could happen. But now I'm
forced to talk resale value and mortgage points. People (People,
you wouldn't believe the bridgemix of people who are now in
my life: my lawyer; my real-estate broker; my mortgage broker.)
have forced me to admit: I want to move in with a boy of the
opposite sex one day, and this place will be too small for that.

So then I have to say, well, it's okay for five years. So suddenly I'm saying: I won't move in with anyone for five years. And then I'm saying back to myself, No, no, no, it doesn't matter, we'll be so in love we'll just squeeze in here together and I'll throw away half my wardrobe and we'll pile his books up to the ceiling in the bathroom. Nutty, right? But I love the stability that this apartment represents. I've been moving every year since I started college. And because my parents split up I haven't had a home base the way some people (like you) do, a place where it's okay to store boxes of books and high school journals. If home, job, and mate are the big three, then at least I can nail down one, by myself, for a good long time. If all goes well, I should close on it and move there in a month or so. Go, I say to roommates, go and never darken my towels again. (Oh, you know I love them, as I loved you, and can't really complain, but phew.)

Tell me, do you really have rats and spiders in your new digs? I could handle bats and roaches, but rats and spiders are scary. I imagine you standing in the doorway of a mud hut, face-to-face with a fist-sized spider. (I guess the spider would have to be dangling from the ceiling.) What I can't picture is some period of activity during which the spider is transformed from a living being to a big, flat, hairy pile. Somehow I just can't see you doing it. Do you scream and wave your arms? Do you call for your manly husband? Do you pull out a cartoon can of Raid and go to town?

Are you teaching yet? Don't you dare become Kenyan citizens and leave me bereft.

More soon, but right now,
Love,
H

Dear Hilary,

For the time being, Kenya has totally kicked both of our butts. Now we are full-time housewives, in a big way. Every day we have to go to market (most food spoils overnight), get water by bicycle, and sweep the omnipresent red dust out of our finally and sweatily conquered house. Every day we cook over charcoal fires, burn the trash, bury the compost, pour our tea-colored water through a coffee filter to get out the chunks, boil it (yes, start the fire again), put it through a ceramic filter, and sometimes wash our clothes. Then perhaps a nice flour and water meal and a sponge bath by candlelight, and we try to sleep through the drumming of the neighbors' Praising the Lord and the shrieks of the bush babies. And now to be teaching too (well, not yet). (As Dave said, the term ends in April, so school probably has to start sometime before that, right?)

We finally met some of our students-to-be this week, and it got us more excited to start teaching because chatting with them was so much fun. They were really shy at first, but when we spoke to them in Kiswahili and were willing to make fools of ourselves doing it, they started to laugh and ask us questions. One boy wanted to know how many cows Dave had traded to marry me. I think he seriously undermined my credibility as a teacher by saying I was free. That probably makes me a prostitute. The kids thought it was very funny. Later, while having tea, Mr. Mbogo, the Islamic studies teacher, asked us if it was really true. When David confirmed it, Mr. Mbogo raised his hands to the sky and said, "Oh God, take me to America, where the women are free!" Anyway, we're hoping classes will begin in earnest next week.

About your vision of me having a face-off with a big spider in a mud hut: I don't live in a mud hut. It's made of concrete. (But there is usually a lot of mud in it tracked in by goats and chickens. The door doesn't close very well.) Upon seeing a spider I mostly walk away and assume she'll be gone by the time I come back. The house feels like home now, although because it's so big mostly the rooms are empty. I keep thinking of that line from "Rumpelstiltskin": "There was nothing in the room but a chair, a spinning wheel, and a heap of straw." Except when I read it in my head I stop after "There was nothing in the room. . . ."

Already, Ramisi is starting to look different to me. At first I could only see the fallen down, ghost-town decay of the place. Then yesterday while coming back from market, I noticed that on some of the houses, the stoops were washed, the clotheslines taut, and the dirt around the front was packed down and its edges neatened. I thought, How clean! Some parts of Ramisi seem downright bright. I think part of it is self-consciousness over the lamb poop on our own doorstep. (Who wants to use precious water cleaning it?) But then again, there are our neighbors to the right. The son, a guy about our age, has something like cerebral palsy, and sits all day and into the night in front of his tumbled-down house looking out over the dying town. He only responds to our greetings with a sort of half look, and then he goes back to staring. He seems like a character from *The Ballad of the Sad Café.*

As for food, yesterday when I saw a shriveled-up carrot for sale in the market I dove on it excitedly. We pick rocks out of the rice like we are supposed to but never get them all, and it would increase your nightmares of losing your teeth. On the bright side, we can now officially add coconut milk to our short but growing list of ingredients. The other night we decided to make coconut rice. We had the coconut, a hammer, and a deadly, serrated, deer-gutting knife we got as a wedding present. I was holding the knife and the coconut while Dave tried to pound it open and hold the tin dish under it to catch the juice. There were a lot of hands and instruments and noise going on, and not a lot of coconut juice. To make it all that much more embarrassing, there were about twenty neighborhood kids staring at us from our doorway (as always since we're such a spectacle), probably thinking we were trying to do a magic trick. To make conversation I said, Hey kids, I can't get the coconut open. Cute little Ali dashed off, and I figured I had scared him, but he soon came back bringing one of our neighbor women whom we hadn't met. She was carrying a huge double-edged sword and looked very determined. I was thinking, Sure, we're having a little trouble here, but you don't have to kill us for it. (Then I thought, Yes, maybe that would be best.) She walked right in, helped herself to our tortured coconut, and with one blow cracked it in half. It was a Wonder Woman moment. Dave is very excited that we will be buying such a manly kitchen instrument. Unfortunately, all the coconut juice went onto the floor when she did it, but who's going to argue with a woman with a *panga?* (This incident has evolved into a friendship, and Mama Abdu has since taught me many cooking tricks, like that coconut milk isn't the whitish water in the center of the nut, it's made from the meat. Who knew!)

It's amazing the different meals Mama Abdu taught me to cook out of just flour and water (and some lard): a hot, liquidy, Cream of Wheat thing for breakfast called *uji,* a congealed lump like polenta (or Play-Doh) for lunch called *ugali,* and a flattened fried patty for dinner, called *chapati.* I felt like I was watching an infomercial for flour.

Last night Dave and I sat on our back stoop and watched the sunset. Yes, we sort of have a wasteland in the backyard, but in the not-so-distant distance, beyond the burnt ground, is some greenery—trees and palmy things, and there's a palm tree right by the house, so we saw the pink and orange sunset, the silhouette of a coconut palm, and a bright planet overhead. We were just sitting there by the charcoal fire, and occasionally a monkey or a jungle chicken would squawk or a sheep would wander over and nose through our compost. Then we had ourselves some warm, flat Coke, and Dave fried up some *chapati,* which he is very good at cooking, and we munched in the toxic incense of mosquito-repellant smoke. Now and then a child running by would yell, "*Habari,* Daudi! *Jambo,* Katie!" Or a man returning from the next-door village would stop and chat with us about the day. We were thinking—hey, this is pretty okay.

But I don't think you need to prepare for us living here permanently. I miss you all too much, and it's too much damn work. Still, I am learning how to do things for the first time, with help from our neighbors, who teach us how to do everything because it's never done the way you might think (the Lesson of the Coconut). I can't just go to the store and get Scotch tape to fix things. If I need to make two items stick together, I have to figure out how to do that with whatever is around—spit, dirt, melted garbage, whatever. My students use thorns as pins to hold their papers together—when they want to hold their papers together. It's nice not to feel the slightest need for plastic wrap. Yes, Hilary, I know plastic wrap prevents a lot of very unsanitary and microbial things from happening. But since a person doesn't die right away from eating food that hasn't been wrapped in plastic (usually), and because thorns seem to work rather well as paper fasteners (when you don't accidentally run your fingers over the corners of your students' papers, leaving a messy dribble of blood), it gives one a feeling of independence.

Of course, I can walk through a magical doorway any second I choose and be back in my American world of

OfficeMax and plastic popper-pins-that-tell-you-when-the-turkey's-done-roasting. So my feeling of independence is really not from deprivation but actually from privilege and wealth. I can feel lighter, relieved of the load of a life of luxury. Poor American me. This is how I make myself sick in my free time—by making sure I realize that I'm lucky to have those things that I'm happy not to have. And for the record (just so it's clear that I am bent on making myself morally miserable) I also think it's ridiculous to believe you have to feel lucky about every staple. No one should really have to appreciate staples. It would just take too long. What I'm saying is that it's okay with me if you go ahead and continue taking your spoiled, rich little life for granted.

Some graffiti in an old schoolbook I found says, "So far as I discovered you are the only girl who has qualification to be centre of my universe." That goes for you, babe.

Still unable to carry anything of consequence atop my head,

Kate

P.S. I have learned that there used to be many large pythons around here when the sugar plantation was active because pythons love sugar. I think you should put that in one of your poems.

Dear Hilary,

Today while we were teaching, the Inspector from the District Headquarters came to check up on all of us teachers. He was a straight-backed old man with a carved walking stick and a full uniform. When Mr. Kasumbi, a teacher notorious for not showing up for class, saw the Inspector approach, he stopped writing on the chalkboard midsentence, looked around him in every direction, and took off running into the jungle. The students in his classroom were giggling and covering their mouths. The Inspector only went to the headmaster's office and then left, so I imagine Kasumbi will get a bit of a ribbing when he comes out from his hiding place.

Yes, as you can see, school has actually started. When I walked into class on the first day, I was definitely nervous, and a little awestruck at the scene in front of me. The classroom has four crumbling and filthy concrete walls that reach halfway to the corrugated tin roof, so it's virtually as if you are still outside. One wall has the remains of a blackboard, although it would be impossible to write a straight line on it because of its holes and lumps. Then, crammed into the back of the room, there are row upon row of grungy, dilapidated desks and chairs, many missing legs or tops, or both. But the most important part, of course, was all the beautiful, eager faces. There are about fifty-five students in one of my form one classes, each in uniform—brown pants or skirt and purple shirt. Everyone must have a shaved head, boys and girls alike. Some of the girls are Muslims, so they wore shining white wraps over their heads. They all were staring at me, of course. Staring is not considered impolite, so they made the most of it. That first day I told them about me and Dave and what we're doing here, began learning their names, and asked them to write the answers to some questions about themselves. They are very, very shy, but my sorry attempts at their names made them smile, so I had hope right from the start that we could connect. (One girl wrote her name on the top of her paper as "Peter's Daughter"!)

A normal Kenyan teacher spends each class hour copying onto the chalkboard notes from his exercise book (which he has copied from some other book) for students to copy into their exercise books. The whole class passes this way, without a sound uttered. The teacher will have a very stern demeanor, and no talking or questions are permitted. Some teachers explain the notes more fully as they go along, but this is not considered necessary. A test will entail regurgitating the copied notes onto the proper blanks on the test. Indiscipline and failure are punished by canings, manual labor, or tauntings.

Can you picture me doing this, Hilary? It pains me. I have all my little plans for group work and developing critical thinking skills, for reading and writing for real purposes, for acting out plays and figuring out the meanings of poems together. Already, my form fours think I am a total fruitcake. They are worried that I am not a serious teacher, because I laugh and try to get them to laugh, because I tell them they have good ideas, because I sometimes say "I don't know" when they ask me a question—a Kenyan teacher no-no—and because I won't cane them. Nonetheless, despite their worries about my leniency, they work with me, they talk with me, they protect me, they teach me. It will be good with them, I think. (Mwasho gave me a little bundle of roasted cashews today, which I'm now eating. He also asked me about a Nike ad he saw in my Peace Corps *Newsweek* that had a picture of a man running into the sky. "Madam, can you get for me some shoes that do that?")

To celebrate our first real week of teaching in Kenya, several of the teachers took us into the "interior" to drink *mnazi,* which is coconut wine. After a mile or two walk in the dark into the jungle, we came to a hut surrounded and lit by flaming coconut husks where we could smell roasting fish. A lot of men were sitting around on small stools. (I can get away with joining the men since I'm so weird anyway.) Everyone was sipping *mnazi* out of old aspirin containers or broken beakers salvaged from some lab's garbage. The straws were made of hollow reeds, each with a wadded up ball of dried grass tied onto the end so that when you sip the *mnazi,* the dead bugs are filtered out. We spent the next five hours drinking and talking about how dangerous lions can be ("Oh they are clever! They will hide behind turnip leaves and if you don't see them they will eat you!"). It was very fun, despite the fact that when we woke up we both felt as though we had ice picks lodged behind our eyes.

Love,

K

P.S. Kate and I just watched helplessly as a baboon grabbed our neighbor's cute little white kitten and took off with it into the jungle. Our neighbor Tibu said the baboon wanted to adopt it since it has no children of its own. Mtua, the little boy who comes with me when I get water sometimes, said that she would eat it. I'm figuring that soon we'll see a cat swinging from tree to tree by vines, or we'll find tiny kitten bones mixed with the mangoes under the tree behind the house.

All the best,

Dave

P.P.S. Kate said to ask you again what you do at your job.

Hidy Kate,

The snow, this paralyzing, post–New Year's megadump, is all
anyone's talking about, and everything is quiet and pretty. It was
a mighty blizzard all right, over two feet of snow. All my crap's
still in storage, and I had to buy snow boots, but since the Gap
has a liberal return policy, I'll be taking them back after I
unpack or after the thaw, whichever comes first. Yesterday was a
snow day for the whole city—the mayor forbade private
vehicles from traveling the streets. So there were zero cars and I
walked down to my dentist in the middle of Fifth Avenue.
Stack is sporting a fake fur coat this season. He refuses to
concede that this makes people think that he is gay. Which he is
not. He wants to write a book on how to act gay to win chicks.
At his suggestion, we played King of the Mountain on the
snow piles. Of course, ladies' man that he is, he let me be king.
Play, I'm even more sure these days, is what we do best.

Right now my whole body is sore from shoveling the walk.
What walk? you say. I've moved. To my new apartment? you
wonder. Ach, well, not yet. I'm staying at a brownstone on the
Upper East Side. It would be really fancy (It belongs to friends
of my parents.) but it's under renovation. The fifth floor, where
I do little more than sleep, is cloaked in sheets of plastic, and
the floors on the way up are coated in a plaster dust that rises

around me as I climb. I pretend I'm the *Flashdance* girl, waving goodbye to construction workers on my way out every morning. But being a nomadic waif in this deserted construction site on Park Avenue is far more palatable than was my dad's loft, particularly when he got up at six to use the NordicTrack two feet from my head.

Clementines are back in season and I'm happy about it. Do you miss them? They are perfect. I thought all of the orange family was great before I ever tasted them. First, the color. Orange is so surreal. Maybe lemon is too—when you think of either color dangling from a tree. Well, I haven't ever seen that, but I have an idea of how surreal it is. So there's the color, and then there's the smell. In *The Shining,* the psychic guy who dies in the movie smells oranges whenever he's about to have a vision. It's a good, strong smell that stays on your fingers. Okay, then there's that white stuff inside an orange peel. It doesn't exist for clementines, but in oranges you can sink your nails into it in a very satisfying way. That's texture. Also, you can light the orange oil on fire or something, right? And clementines peel beautifully, and divide out into perfect sections, and you can see that they are full of juice. And then you eat. And that's a whole nother thing.

On New Year's Eve I brought home a guy I met that night, and, luckily, he isn't an ax murderer and there's even a chance that we'll like each other. He went to Yale and was friends with jocks but has since acquired an all-black outfit to complement his new literary scene. We had our second date (thanks in advance for being generous enough to count New Year's Eve) last night. Maybe it should be fundamental, but I took great pleasure in what felt like a really even exchange. He talked. I talked. He laughed. I laughed. He walked me through the tall snowdrifts to my door, and I thought: I would like to know more about how the world appears to this person. I will invite his lanky, ponytailed self in, up all the stairs, and into my room, which is dominated by the bed. We were looking at Animals of Our National Parks through the Viewfinder that Stack gave me for Christmas when Nick kissed me.

Here's where I feel a little sorry for you. You, my friend, you'll never date again, never dress for a night wondering if he's got a shoe fetish or if he prefers blondes. Never will you wonder if you're attractive and entertaining enough for him until the minute you see him, at which point you will begin to wonder if he's attractive and entertaining enough for you. Never will you negotiate the still-lingering politics of who pays the bill. Never again will you contemplate the first kiss, wondering if it will be cautious or impassioned. It must be a drag to have all that in the past.

My friend's sister is coming to stay with me again for the week. She called last night when Nick, whom I like to call New Year's Guy, and I were making out. I picked it up after fifty rings and was like I can't talk now and she was like, okay, but did I leave my blue jacket there? Arg. Later Nick and I curled in bed together, eating, you guessed it, clementines. As it happened, last night I didn't sleep well because of my snow-shoveling trauma—pitiful, I know. Nick didn't seem to mind my tossing and turning (wink, wink). It's too soon to say what will happen, but luck and lust already prevail in this new year. My mother would definitely disapprove of bed-sharing on a second date, but I feel a need to vary my speed, you know?

Speaking of which, it appears that my brother and Emily will soon join you and Dave on the cruise-control highway. The likely possibility that they will marry delights me. First of all, it locks in Emily as my friend, if not sister. Sister! It's just that I've never gotten to refer to someone as my sister before. Also, it means that Steven won't be co-opted into a distant world of marriage. After all, I picked Emily for him. I've known her for longer than he has. It will just make our family bigger, which we could stand. Those Thanksgivings with just me, Mom, and Steven have been feeling pretty small. Third, I'm sure they'll continue to be as sickeningly in love as they have been. And, gross as they are, at least they still sustain fairly separate personalities. I'm happy. I'm happy for them and for me. I can only imagine the less-than-ideal alternative—that Steven or you might've married people toward whom I had to be polite. Phew. It makes me want my mate to pass your inspection. Oh, and most important, if this goes through I'll get tons of attention and credit for introducing them. My people call that a mitzvah. It really has made me start thinking, Marriage? I can handle marriage if my big brother can, and if you can, and all those other strangers can. But I'll never wear a white dress.

White makes me look green. I might need to get married in the desert, naked.

I went to see a movie with the two of them after we were talking about their pending engagement. When it was over, Steven had to use the men's room and Emily told him not to go, because she wanted to head straight home. He frowned his Charlie Brown frown and I said, "Emily! If you want to marry my brother you'd better not plan to control when he goes to the bathroom! Geez." Steven said, "Yeah. You're not the boss of me," which is what he used to say to me when we were kids. She flushed and giggled and said, "It's so annoying. He always does this." But I made her promise out loud, "I will never stop Steven from heeding nature's call." What would he do without me?

I don't understand about the chunky water? I'm guessing that those chunks aren't Everlasting Gobstoppers. So what, pray tell, enhances your drinking water so meatily? Do you think the teachers were teasing you about the lions? I don't want any uncaged lions to happen to you.

I feel sick from eating too much chocolate. Some things never change. Okay, it's snowing again and I'm going to dinner now with my new work friend. Happy happy new year.

—H

P.S. I'm bad for not having sent this yet. There is so much gossip it's almost not worth your time. Oh weakness, oh repetitiveness, oh curse of ages, I know you don't want to hear it but I slept

with that cad Jason again, but give me credit! I held to my
resolution. I didn't sleep with him one single time last year.
Nick is only a maybe, but so many options! So much
possibility! I must have a good haircut or else it's a hormone.
But I know, I know. I need my adventures to be more than boy-
safaris.

All my love to you and that constipated husband of yours,

Hilary

Oh hello Hilaryish One,

Snow, you say? Snow? Ha, ha, ha, HA—I laugh at the likes of
snow, I laugh at anyone who doesn't laugh at the likes of snow.
What's kind of amazing about how hot I am right now is that
even if I were about to die of heat, there is absolutely not one
thing I can do to make myself any cooler even by a small
fraction of a degree. Sweat and water do nothing because it is so
humid there is little to no evaporation happening. I'm already
virtually naked. Nothing in the whole village is below room
temperature, seeing as there's no refrigeration or air-
conditioning, so there'll be no Snapple had and no place to
cool off. I'm sitting here, sweat running down my face
unchecked (I'd have to wash anything I'd wipe it with) reading
a letter from you about snow and it's not cooling me down. At
all. In fact I'm getting all worked up. Nice. Another cool thing
(oh how ironic) to keep in mind is that I presently have a slight
fever because of my recent case of malaria which is adding a
flush to my crimson cheeks. I just ate a melted Cadbury's Dave
got me in Mombasa when we were last there to save my
malaria-threatened life (I can joke about it since I'm still
alive), which we mightn't have bothered about seeing as
how I'm about to perish of sunstroke, and now the chocolate
is boiling and frothing in my stomach. But a body can't just

let a Cadbury's sit there, as you have taught me. So, in sum, I'm fairly miserable for the moment, although still chatty, much to Dave's resentment as he tries to read the book he recently got in the mail from Uncle Billy (*Dune,* aptly). And how are you?

Yes, about the water. We are currently a bit troubled about our water, seeing as it's the color of shit and smells like the *Exxon Valdez,* so Peace Corps is sending in a bit of it for a test, to find out what those chunks are made of. For now, to get the water, Dave fills up a big vat from a pump a few kilometers away, straps it to his bike, and brings it here. Then, we boil it over a fire and pour it into a ceramic filter inserted in a bucket. We used to use paper filters first to keep the ceramic one from clogging, but our neighbors took us to better water at a different hole, so we don't have to anymore.

I don't think I really knew what canned food was for before. I never realized what an important and amazing invention it is. If it weren't for cans, people in some places could only eat the food they could grow or kill. I mean, if you try to bring anything from anywhere it spoils immediately in the heat. Anyway, a fringe benefit is that now Dave and I have a can that used to contain cheese affixed to the wall of our bathroom with a candle in it so we can see the various infections on our bodies when we wash ourselves after dark. (Did you get that part about canned food? It's important.)

.   .   .

I'm quite worried about the situation at school. I know I started to tell you about this already, but the three weeks since classes have started have really opened our eyes to another whole world of trouble. Despite all that we had read and learned about corruption in Kenya, we had no idea what to expect. Public school costs money here, enough, in fact, that a good many Kenyans can't afford any formal education. Some families or villages pool their money to send just one promising son or daughter to school. This makes it all the more painful to watch when that money seems to disappear into thin air.

In Ramisi, the students have not received any supplies. Without books or paper, following the national curriculum is quite difficult, as you can imagine. Then keep in mind that the headmaster just purchased a new white pickup truck. He seems quite content and doesn't seem too curious about where all the supposedly ordered supplies might be. Everyone tells us that this is the situation all over Kenya, but there doesn't seem to be any way to fight it. The headmaster brings a big fat chicken to the one man in the village who is higher in command than himself, so the two of them are the best of friends.

A few days ago, when the students began to grumble about the situation, the headmaster put the form fours in charge of the younger students, told them he would give them each an exercise book if they would "supervise," and left town. The older students took that to mean they should beat up the younger ones. We arrived at the school to see one of my form four students force a younger one to kneel and then slap him across the face. As this happened, students started to yell and run, and fighting broke out everywhere. We stood there, frozen. Kamango, a teacher friend, suddenly appeared, ripped a big branch off a mango tree, and started flailing it around to break up the fighting. The boys ran off yelling. After we cleared up the broken desks and chairs, Kamango walked us the short way home and told us that if the rumbling started again, we should join him in leaving town, since students in situations like these sometimes become violent with teachers.

Now, a day later, occasional screams across the courtyard (which can be normal coming from a crowd of teenagers) set my heart beating hard until I hear quiet again. To tell the truth, what's hardest to understand is that the other teachers and neighbors don't seem shocked by the fighting. They talk to us about the dangers of incidents like this, but if nothing happens on Monday, I have the feeling that everyone is going to pretend it never occurred. I feel like people should be horrified and should show it. They should not think this is okay or normal, even if they are used to it. It is a big deal that the students are being mistreated, that they have been robbed and beaten, and now it's another big deal that they are beating each other. Maybe people are embarrassed to act as if it's significant in front of us outsiders. Maybe they want us to dismiss it, so they are acting like it is something that can be dismissed. More likely, though, people are too used to it to get worked up.

On another front: I will not speak about you re-sleeping with the unspeakable one. I have crossed it out of your letter

and it will not be spoken about. He is Wrong and Bad and you
will Stop. Don't think you can do it just because I am so far
away, either. *No.* Bad, Hilary, bad dog! *No!* The other one,
Nick, seems okay so far, but you would know what I'd think
about him better than I would, at this point. Congratulate
Steven and Emily for me.

Although I neatly ripped off this section of paper, thinking I
had exactly that much more to say, I now find that my
chattiness has succumbed to my sluggishness. In other words,
there is no more.

(Except)
Love,
Kate

Hi Kate,

Oh, favorite person, if you lived here then I would see you. Oh
my God this fancy computer is capitalizing the first letters of
my sentences. Geez. Also it puts a red wavy line under words
like *Kate* and *geez*. Let this luxurious high-tech extravaganza
stand in contrast to your current situation. I'd (it capitalized that
too) say that you are experiencing the passage of time more
slowly than I am. Weeks fly here and it seems to me that I write
you a letter, then I get one, then I write one. My life is moving
very fast, and it's all pretty fluid. But I think that you are doing a
million new things every day and learning a whole life. I have
trouble actually reacting to the peril of your situation. It's as if
you've gone to war. And I'm here just finishing my peppermint
pattie. Mmmm. Remember peppermint patties?

　I sort of expected that you would get malaria. I bet you hid it
from everyone for ten years too. Typical. Just don't get Ebola
because then you'll liquefy from the inside out and that would
be totally gross. Your most recent letter really made me
appreciate temperature regulation. You know how kids like to
ask: would you rather freeze to death or burn to death? Guess
you have an answer now. I won't tease you by reminding you of
how dramatically cold movie theaters are in the summer here.
It's nothing a nice toasty fire and some hot chocolate wouldn't

help. Mostly, I can't imagine you in a place without showers, considering that they are your sanity mainstay. Kate, without an hour-long shower for meditation and ritual detoxification? This will truly test your mettle. Your situation seems worse than it's supposed to be. If it's so hard to accomplish anything, are your struggles worth it? You sound so hot and dirty. I'm counting on those prenatal vitamins to keep you scurvy-free. But I'm worried about the malaria, or is it the common cold of Africa? You'll come home if it's too bad, right? Could you please be serious for one minute about this? I'm not your mother. Don't give me sunshine and petunias. I'll be angry at you if you send me a bunch of blasé letters and then drop dead.

It's Presidents' Day but I'm in the office. Busy, as you can see. My eyes hurt. I don't love my job but my boss, Cindy (she gets mad about being called "boss"), is very cool and we keep working as we power-walk down the halls and even when we're in the bathroom stalls and when I told my grandfather that he said, "Now I'm worried. Are you both straight?" I wasn't quite sure how to respond. I didn't even know he knew the word *straight* meant anything other than not crooked.

I think my plan will work. I keep having to remind myself that I don't have to do it forever, and that my learning curve is high. Although this job isn't ideal, it's what they call a career move. But the commute to Westchester is brutal, and I do it at least three days a week. The rest of the time I'm in the Soho office. The company is Kafkaesque. I'm still totally unsettled, confused, have no real definition of what my job is, and yet am busy all the time. I'm getting a reputation for excusing myself from meetings abruptly, but if I didn't I wouldn't be able to accomplish a thing. I'm a little tired of trying to explain what I do, but what's surprising is how much fun I'm having. When we're not in meetings, the office I share with Cindy is something of a social gathering area. Who knows why? We always have to send our work friends away so we can be productive. It reminds me of how I used to study in the library at college. You know how I like that. Pretending to try to work.

That New Year's guy Nick, who was in the Number One spot, fell off the board entirely last week when we had drinks and he told me that his ex-girlfriend to whom he hasn't spoken since they fought and broke up five months ago called him and they met up and were fighting and he kissed her. As he was telling me that he needed time to figure all this out, it became all the more clear to me that he's perfect! (Just kidding.) My question is, why, why, why have I been designated long-term ambassador for the lonely? That's me, I venture out into foreign lands, negotiate, cajole, support the needs of both sides (him and me); I've tried scrubbing, even spraying, still . . . Nick is a perfect example of . . . of whatever it is that I do wrong or the world does wrong to me. A few days ago we were walking through deep snowdrifts. I was wearing a colorful scarf; he was making me laugh; and I felt like the apple-cheeked happy girl, the one who sometimes has a boyfriend and sometimes does not but is always cheered by hope and possibility. And then, mere hours later—not even enough time for me to blame myself—I am in a bar having a "talk," and saying to him, "So it's all bad timing, right? . . . Right?" I'm saying that and I'm thinking, All over the world men are leaving their old girlfriends for new girlfriends, but not right here in Orson's Bar. Nope, not Orson's. In Orson's it goes the other way. It's not that I'll miss him. I barely knew him. But it makes me sad that we never got to the breakfast in bed part, the Sunday crossword on Saturday night part. When I have a nightmare I want to be able to fling my arm around a safe body. I want there to be one person who knows me better than anyone else. Is that so wrong? (No, Kate, thanks, but you don't count. It needs to be a mutually exclusive thing.)

I know that you are hot and being slowly poisoned by drinking oil. Even so, what you have to concede is that couples have it better under all circumstances. Being single means carrying groceries home, eating them, reading, and eventually falling asleep and waking up and doing it all again. But when you're in a couple you carry groceries together. Someone slices while you dice; someone sits on the toilet lid to talk while you brush; and when you settle down to read, someone's leg flops over your leg, a reminder that you are attractive, that you are loved, that even in your solitary activities someone is considering you, that life has meaning. Not only am I alone every night, but I actively, painfully miss my yet-unfound Dave every day as if he were lost at sea.

Don't get me wrong. I am full of joy. Even in my disappointment, my youthful exuberance persists. Depression is a stranger to me. Love is an accordion. And yes, sigh, even though Nick is gone I know there are others. This includes, I'm ashamed to admit, Jason the heartbreaker, whom I slept with just one more time, which, when coupled with the last time, had the effect of giving a single event a second dimension. That is, once there are two points there is a line and once there is a line there is a visible direction and once there is direction there is desire and that's why I have to quit. What can I say? I'm a sucker for a scruffy drummer with a four a.m. bedtime. But I hadn't yet gotten your letter forbidding me to mention or interact with him. I take your orders. I am resolved and don't feel that it will be too difficult. And, last and least on the boy report, Byron was quoted as having said that going out with me was like going out with a man. Apparently he believes that he cooked and cleaned and made us a home and that I took it all for granted. Eve told him: You're just saying that because Hilary is the only woman you've ever respected and you don't know how to express it. Byron agreed.

My malarial African friend, are you going to contract weird diseases where giraffes explode out of your skin? Are you wearing hats constantly I hope? What do you use your electric outlet for? Do you have a TV? (Trivial, I know.) Are you having the same experience as Dave or different experiences? Is one of you happier? Is one of you dirtier? How is all this hardship affecting your married life? Are you ever homesick so that you want to cry?

I miss you both just terribly and am working very hard to

make sure the world keeps turning so that winter turns to summer and summer turns back to winter and then it all happens again or another half a time and then you're back. At this point you are using up so much of my love supply that wars might start. Luckily, you're working for the Peace Corps, so no one's getting too rambunctious. Happy Valentine's Day, sweethearts.

—H

Hi Hilary,

Why, oh why does everyone who writes me expect that Dave
and I will have begun fighting now that we're married and in
Kenya? We haven't. Not in the least. In fact, the only thing we
ever fought about has been eliminated since here it's too hot for
covers. There is one thing that drives us apart, which is the fact
that Dave laughs every time I fart (not funny) (probably a sign
of a serious disease). And that he keeps bringing up the fact that
once, in New York, when picking out food for dinner, I claimed
that I only liked *black* beans. As you know, this is not really a
very appropriate attitude considering our current bean selections.
In all truthfulness, we're closer than ever. I love being here with
David.

I now wear a slip when I teach. I am the T.O.D. this week
(that would be Teacher on Duty). That means I have to fill out
a bunch of papers every day for various reasons, like: student
needs to wear *pata patas* instead of regulation footwear because
she has a "wound" on her foot, or student needs to leave school
to get paraffin to burn for light to study by, or student must go
to a tailor because her skirt is ripped. I am the one who is
supposed to open each morning with a speech about how
poorly the kids are measuring up, and I am the one who is
supposed to whip them all with a cane for infractions. The

week began with the headmaster putting the stripped bamboo cane on my desk in the staff room. He knows I'm not going to touch it.

We got a nice letter from our Peace Corps boss that read thus: "Hi Kate and Dave, Kate I hope you are feeling better. FYI we got the technician's report on your filtered, treated drinking water and it read 'Unfit for Human Consumption.' See attached. We'll see!" Wouldn't that mean to you that we have no safe drinking water? And wouldn't it bespeak of problems? It's ironic since otherwise they've taken incredibly good care of us medically. They taught us everything from how to grind up eggshells for calcium to how to keep ourselves protected from the AIDS virus, which, in Nairobi, one in ten people have. We'll have to take a trip into the city to see what's going on. I don't want to have two-headed babies or to continue being sick all the time.

When we shared the "Unfit for Human Consumption" report and the chemical breakdown of the water in the staff room (in it are fecal material from a nearby *choo* and pesticides left from the sugar plantation), the other teachers' interest soon turned to semijokes about it being "unfit for *white man's* consumption." The general tone was that everyone's been drinking the water with no problem for ten years and now we come in with Western technology and say it's not okay, that they have to spend lots of money to change, what could be done about it anyway, and, really, even if it was radioactive and had mercury and lead in it, "we'd drink it if we got thirsty." Yet another Kate-and-Dave-only crisis. I get so frustrated! Things could be done—if not moving the *choo,* trucking in water (it happens a lot in the drier areas), or digging a new borehole, couldn't we at least boil the water for the students who live at the school? Especially since there have been numerous problems with diarrhea outbreaks and stomachaches? But no, we are told the children are fine. It's tricky to be telling people that their ways aren't good enough. I don't know if they don't want to hear it from us whites, if they don't want to contest "God's will," or if they just don't care. We're telling our students to boil the water themselves, but the fuel costs money, so they probably can't.

Just now I had my glass of said water in the form of hot tea that's about half sugar and a quarter yellowy, uddery milk. Nice on a 104-degree day. But I also had some fried cassava with salt and hot red pepper which was excellent.

About Jason: oh, Hilary.

About Nick: oh, Nick.

And by the way, *are* you and your boss both straight? (*Unlike* Josh Stack?) And what relation at all does that have with talking about work in the bathroom? Or is your grandpappy just a little off his loop? And talking about your friends at work does not count as telling me what you do. I'm beginning to think you work for the CIA.

Oh Hilary, you might be interested to know that to celebrate the end of the fasting and praying of Ramadan, our neighbors invited us over for goat, mango gravy, and Jell-O substitute.

Shabina, who is sixteen and not allowed out of the house (even for schooling) because she might have sex, decorated my hands in the traditional Swahili way by making designs with henna on my palms so that I sort of look like Dax on *Deep Space Nine* except it's not on my forehead and it will come off in a month or so. She's really quite talented at it. When we got over there, I was immediately whisked into the kitchen with the women to decorate ourselves, chat, and munch tasty treats as we cooked. Dave told me later that the men slaughtered the goat (!), drank homebrew (known to cause blindness), ate piles of unripe mangoes with hot pepper on them (known to cause digestive trouble), and sprayed each other with a cockroach killer called DOOM (known to cause neurological damage) to repel insects. Isn't it nice to be a girl?

Just so that you can picture my hand completely, I lost my wedding ring in the dirty laundry water that we dump in the *choo*. We got another ring that is brass and lots of other women wear them with no trouble because they have black skin so their adjoining fingers don't turn an alarming shade of green. On the same hand, along with the henna patterns, brass ring, green smudges, and calluses, I now have a nice blistery rash like poison ivy, which we finally learned is caused by eating cashew nuts that are not all the way cooked or by standing in the smoke while they are roasting. Both of which we, naively, did.

Kariuki, a teacher, just asked if we had ever studied Descartes and I tried desperately to remember your joke about him, but I can't.

To answer your trivial question (you are forgiven), the man who owns the wrecked sugar factory is the only one who has a TV. Therefore, the electricity comes on when there's a show he wants to watch, but now the generator's broken. That means the village hasn't gathered around the screen lately, and maybe won't ever again. Another sign of Ramisi's slow decay.

While riding our bikes home, we were stopped by a guy with a bow and arrow who asked which way the baboon went, then shook our hands and ran off. As will I now.

Love,

K

Hil,

Right now it's evening and the entire acre-square courtyard, the center of Ramisi, is burning. Smoke is blowing through our house, and the firelight is lighting the room instead of a lantern. Shabina told us it's necessary to burn the grass down every so often to keep away the poisonous snakes and mosquitoes.

Things here are hell, as usual; we can't quite believe how bad it is. We're in a daze. The chores aren't so draining now that the neighbors have explained the best way to do things and we've done them a few times. The school's repression and badness-for-kids, however, is, so far, unabating (is that a word?). I mean, although it seems it cannot go on like this, it has been able to and may continue to. Doctors have it easy, I think. If a person is bleeding, everyone agrees that the wound has to be treated. Without blood or pus to indicate a universally accepted problem, what am I supposed to do here? What I see as a wound to be treated, like polluted water or a dependence on the cane in the classroom, no one else I know sees as a problem. Peace Corps says we are invited here by the Kenyan government to help in the way Kenyans want us to help. In this case, that's following their lead, teaching their syllabus, in their way. Peace Corps says it's arrogant and irresponsible and maybe even colonialist to decide to do anything else. But there's just no way I'm going to spend two years here teaching kids to sit down and shut up and accept whatever stupidly unfair situations are imposed on them by people with big sticks.

Today Khadija and Amina, two of my form fours, tried to strangle a third girl they suspected of squealing on them as ringleaders of last week's walkout. Quite probably, some teachers are thinking that this has occurred since I wouldn't cane anyone this week, although I of course attribute it to the fact that the students are constantly abused. The girls are at the police station right now. Mohammed voiced concerns initially that the police would be too brutal on them (which says a lot since he canes them pretty hard), but other teachers decided that would be good discipline. Jesus H. Christ is about all I say about school nowadays—it applies most of the time.

In fact, the whole situation is beginning to make me crazy. I feel myself talking too much and too loudly when I think about it. I feel jittery and, when in the house, cry easily. I think it's because Dave and I feel so strongly that what is going on is horrible, and everyone around us thinks it's just fine. Of course, it's all about what a person is raised to believe, it could all be called culture, but I wasn't raised to believe this, and I can't be open-minded about it. Maybe I should say that I don't want to be open-minded about it. Cultural assimilation is all fine and good when it's about not having electricity, eating unfamiliar food, and gesturing for people to come nearer with your palm facing down, not up, but abusing those "below" you is something else entirely. And on top of that, I don't know if this stuff is really Kenyan culture or the culture left over from British colonialism, or culture created by poverty and hopelessness. You see how I rant and rave these days?

The end of the term is approaching, so we'll go by bus to the northern border, where we'll take a boat and go to an island. And drink and eat and walk on the beach. And try to grow some sanity back.

Love,
Kate

P.S. Here is a poem we're studying that I copied for you:

THE BELOVED
by A. R. Cliff-Lubin

Lapobo,
Tall but not too tall,
Short but not too short,
She is of medium size.

Lapobo,
Her teeth are not as ash,
Nor the color of maize flour,
Her teeth are white as fresh milk.
The whiteness of her teeth
When I think of her
Makes food drop from my hand.

Lapobo,

Black but not too black,

Brown but not too brown,

Her skin is just between black and brown.

Lapobo,

Her heels have no cracks.

Her palms are smooth and tender to touch.

Her eyes—Ho they can destroy anybody.

Descartes walks into a bar.

Bartender says: Would you like a beer?

Descartes says: I think not, and, poof! he disappears.

Dear K8,

I'm pretty angry about your water situation. In my world, you'd ask your director what she plans to do about the report that says it's "unfit for human consumption" and cc: her boss. This is how working for a big company with a stagnant company culture has made me think (and did I ever talk about "company culture" before this job?). But you must take action on this.

As you probably anticipated, my favorite part of the poem you sent me is the tall but not too tall part. (I just remembered you were sort of in my dream—there was someone that I saw from the back and I was like I think that's Kate but then I thought, No it couldn't be, she's in Africa. So you see you're even too far away for dreams. Trippy, huh?) So with these dire circumstances, do you feel like your energies are worth it? I mean, you and Dave are very valuable resources, not to mention people, and I think you should only suffer if there's at least some payoff for the community. Then again, that which does not kill you makes you stronger. But make sure you keep evaluating this, since we (those who love you) can't do so from here.

Speaking of our "company culture," some of it isn't so stagnant. Don't get the idea that I'm into computers because I am a hundred percent not. I'm a nature lover with a log-cabin fantasy. Please don't forget that. Anyway, at work we can do this thing on the computers called instant messaging. It's as fast as talking on the phone, but you're typing on the computer. Losers like my boss, Cindy (who, like me, is straight, thank you very much), and me, and my new work friend Keith (who gets mad when I call him that because he claims that we are friend friends) all sometimes do this with each other and we just crack up. It's like discovering the pleasure of passing notes in high school. (It's just so funny, but I realize I should probably save this "humor" for my autobiography, which I intend to call *You Had to Be There.*) Even though Cindy and I share an office where we sit back to back, sometimes she'll instant-message me. She could just turn around and talk. Then she'll call me on the phone, which is totally ridiculous, so I'll type, "I'm not answering that" and "Cut it out." Do you see how infantile this is? For some reason it makes us weep with silent laughter. My chat "handle" is "luckyh," and Cindy and Keith and a few other work friends sometimes call me Lucky, which I like. It's like in college, when I changed my mantra from "my life is hell" to "I have a lust for life" and things got better. If they just call me Lucky long enough maybe I'll actually get lucky.

I had dinner with Delia last night and she couldn't believe that I wear panty hose to work. She said that she can't stand hose and would never do that. Of course Delia's an actress and gets to wear red polka-dotted skirts and little tee shirts whenever she wants. I was vaguely annoyed that she doesn't understand that I do this because, unlike her, I have to support myself. I explained to her that I've now been so exposed to office wear that I think it looks bad to wear a suit without panty hose. While we were having this trivial exchange, it dawned on me that since I've become a working girl I have broken many of the promises we made to ourselves in college: never to wear panty hose or painful shoes, never to have manicures, never to dye my hair or wear makeup every day or pay more than twenty dollars for a haircut or carry a purse. Little by little I've caved in to this time-consuming self-maintenance, originally in an effort to be taken seriously. Now I do some of it because I'm actually becoming part of office culture, not to mention beauty culture. I get manicures because I don't think I have especially pretty hands but every time I have my nails done some man compliments them. I think it's silly, but eight bucks for a compliment is a bargain. Still, I worry about what this is doing to me. When I started my first job, I remember having a separate work persona, which I couldn't reconcile with my home life. Now those two personas have pretty much merged. I am officially a working stooge. I know there was a reason I kept those two lives separate, but now I'm not even sure of what I have sacrificed. As a working girl what can't I do or think? It seems that as the years pass, conformity will fester and spread. I won't be able to talk about anything beyond movies and the latest celebrity scandal. But the terrifying part is the idea that those things will feel like the most vibrant issues.

My primary concern these days (on the road to Blandville) is my new digs. My apartment purchase is finally happening, so I will probably leave my bulldozed tower soon. Last week I went by the apartment for a final inspection (you know, to make sure the previous owners didn't steal the light fixtures—which they didn't—or the towel racks—which they did). My broker was schmoozing with the doorman and I was left alone in the apartment. The electricity was off, but there was a warm light coming in from the hall. I stood there thinking, I can't believe I own a whole refrigerator. (I know you're thinking I have no idea of how amazing refrigeration is.) And my refrigerator, which is mine that I own, will only host food that appeals to me. People I care about will visit, and make poems out of Magnetic Poetry on it. I stood in the living room and thought, I'm going to see the light through different seasons here. I'm going to play music and do my dishes and fold my laundry. I'm going to order in sushi and read *The New Yorker.* I felt so easy, so content right then. I had to refrain from doing a little dance. But I will—I will do funny dances, and I will talk to myself. This, I told myself, is more than just a box I've checked off some list of needs. I'm an American! I own land! (Well, in a way.) What good walls! A whole world that I will make mine in its cleanliness (or lack thereof). I can't wait.

But of course everything is crazy because I close on

Thursday, Friday I paint, then I have to go to DC for the weekend because Steven wants to talk to our grandfather about his engagement. That would be my grandfather's engagement, not Steven's! This is all happening not even a year after my grandmother's death. Steven wants to make sure my grandfather knows that we're here to help and that he's sort of vulnerable and shouldn't get married out of fear or dependence. Because it came up so suddenly and without discussion, Steven's sort of panicked about it. Have you ever seen Steven upset? It's disconcerting, because he's usually so placid. I'm used to being the unsettled one. He's thinking a lot about family these days—getting engaged and all. I think being so close to Emily also allows him to compare his own family with the workings of another. I'm definitely concerned about my grandfather and agree that we should make sure he knows that we love him and can help him. But I think that Steven is feeling that all marriages should be based on the same values he and Emily have in their relationship. It's not quite the same when you're in your eighties, newly widowed, and unable or unwilling to cook or drive or clean or run a house. The whole thing makes me miss my grandmother, and mostly it'll be exhausting.

And then Monday my jailed belongings will finally be set free. I'm going skiing in Salt Lake so I have to unpack and find all my ski stuff right away. The ski trip is with Dad, Steven and Emily. Then Dad's mate, Genevieve, and her friend will be in the same area but a separate condo. We were all supposed to be together, but now my dad and Genevieve are having relationship troubles so we're going semiseparated because Dad didn't want to let us down and Genevieve didn't want to let her friend down. How insane (albeit kind) is that. . . . As you can see, my family's a little messy these days.

And how are you, my heroic missionary? Saving the world? When I think about it, it's painfully obvious that not once did my parents say: Young Hilary, you gotta put something back in the pot. Is that strange to you? I was reared to be a good friend but not a good citizen. They say charity begins at home, so I guess that makes me a beginner. And in order to have a home in which to be charitable, I have to pay my mortgage. But Kate, isn't it nice to know that so long as I pay my bills, there is a place in New York City that is totally safe and welcoming, always, for me, and you, and even that African husband of yours? I will give you a key, just in case you're on Seventh Avenue and you get a blister. My adhesive bandages are your adhesive bandages. And with that generous declaration, love and goodbye.

XOXOXO,
Hilary

Hil,

I'm glad to see you are at least being honest and reflective about totally selling out. I love you anyway.

The other day we had a bounty from heaven—it rained! It was the middle of the night and we both woke with a rush of adrenaline. Did we have enough buckets out to catch it? What other containers could we find? Quick! We collected 344½ liters! When we bathed, we washed our feet, and for the first time in months, rinsed the last little bit of soap from our hair. And you wouldn't believe all the laundry we did! We thought we were sitting pretty—enough clean water to sink a battleship. Now, three days later, all the buckets in the house are still full, but an outside observer would probably think we were doing experiments in swamp ecosystems instead of accumulating a drinking water supply. I never would have thought it possible for such things to grow in the clean-looking, drained-off-our-roof, bleached water. I'm not even sure we should call it water anymore. Oh well. We had to sterilize all our filter equipment in boiling caldrons, and Dave biked home a backpack full of bottled Fanta to hold us over. Imagine being really, really, really thirsty and having to choose between stagnant pond scum water or orange syrup to drink.

The other morning I was rolling around under the mosquito

net trying not to feel guilty about Dave already being awake and puttering around when suddenly I heard this stifled gasp/scream/ curse from the other room. I said to myself, What happened? (But I said it really slowly because I was just waking up.) And I thought maybe Dave by accident stepped in the fire he was making to cook me an egg and mango juice breakfast in bed. Not bloody likely. Maybe, as we had both foretold, he had actually finally succeeded in killing a chicken with his breath, but there was no squawking. I was just turning over to have a nice dream about apples and cheese when Dave came running in all worked up because some kind of a poisonous snake dropped on his neck. Sure enough, it kept slithering around our steps. Since ninety percent of the snakes around here are deadly poisonous, I was thinking that someone really should do something about it. We had a short debate about whether a snake could slither up a stick that was jabbing it and bite the person holding it, but I decided that Dave should go ahead and give it a try. So, in a very manly fashion, he poked it to death. After it was dead, and looking a lot more like a baby snake, we decided that (a) it wasn't a black mamba and that (b) it probably wouldn't have killed us instantly unless it had highly poisonous gums. So it lay there with its pale belly up, the chickens ate at it, and we felt a little quiet. The poor guy probably munched on mosquitoes and bread crusts, maybe a potato peel now and then. I bet he liked warm rocks and even had a stamp collection.

Kate

P.S. You should know that the snake with the stamp collection was two and a half feet long, as thick as my arm, mean-looking, and landed on my neck! I did not "poke" him to death. I slew that sucker, and saved both of our lives. And probably the lives of our neighbors too.

Dave

Dear K8,

It's April 10th. I sent you a postcard yesterday. But you deserve more, oh yes. I'm back from skiing in Utah. Going on vacation with my father was like meditating to a car alarm. He was extremely concerned with getting to the slopes on time, or where something should go in the kitchen (I was like, it's a rental. Put the bowl wherever you want), or where we should ski the next day. And in the mornings, the more impatient my father got, the more Steven seemed to slow down. But as soon as we got out to the mountains we did pretty well, for a family.

I don't know how to break this to you gently, so here it is, plain: I lost my cybervirginity last week. I figured it was part of working for an online company, market research and all. It's so weird: there are chat rooms with names like Love Shack where the lascivious lurk, saying things like, Any hot girls in the room? Most people are either obnoxious and gross or they're from Kentucky and want to treat a lady like a lady. This is what I learned in the space of a few hours. So I was flirting with two guys at the same time (as you know, I'm a pretty fast typist). Both were twenty years old (or so they said, everyone lies about everything). One was dumb as a tree but really sweet. He kept apologizing and making smiley faces like this :). The dopey nice guy couldn't spell and I hated him, but turns out it's just as hard to get rid of losers in chat as it is in real life. Meanwhile the other was a hard-core whacker named PUKED, which gives you an idea of how sophisticated he was, but who cares? None of it's real. So I toyed around with those guys for a while. Believe me, you don't want the details. I know you think you do. Okay, it's like phone sex, except that you're typing your fantasies. Anyway, let's just say I had virtual sex with a man who was probably a lousy lay but an okay typist. I didn't have to worry about how I looked, whether we loved each other, birth control, or whether he'd stay for breakfast. I thought, I could get used to this.

A while later I found myself wanting to see whether I could get something else going (I was bored, okay?), and I started talking to KingX. KingX seemed just my type—a cynical, bored TV writer who worked in Soho. He was the only typist who seemed capable of proper use of the apostrophe. "Tell me a secret or I'm leaving," he said. The very possibility that I might be boring him was so intolerable that I decided to let him in on my transformation: "I lost my cybervirginity tonight," I told him. He seemed so normal that I was totally scared to talk dirty to him because I was terrified that he'd turn out to be someone I know. Like my *brother* or something. An awful thought. But then, as he questioned me about the cybersex, I found my image of him to be magically evolving into that of the ideal stranger.

We segued seamlessly into a shared fantasy—it started with him typing, "What are you wearing?" And me admitting my less-than-sexy flannel pajamas. He claimed that flannel was sexy but was soon standing behind me and helping me remove it. I can't bring myself to tell you exactly what happened, but, since you insist, I'll include an excerpt, so you know how it goes.

LUCKYH: where are you, at a desk?
KINGX: yeah, you?
LUCKYH: I'm on my bed.
KINGX: ?
LUCKYH: laptop
KINGX: of course
LUCKYH: what are you wearing?
KINGX: boxers
LUCKYH: that's all?
KINGX: afraid so
LUCKYH: take them off
KINGX: if you say so . . .
KINGX: they're off.

His language was too much like a trashy romance for my taste ("I slide my hands down your soft skin"), but, in a way I never could have on dry land, I let it go.

It's amazing how enlightening a change of medium can be. In the real time of the moment I found myself saying (typing) exactly what came to mind, without processing for taste or dignity or precision. I used words with this stranger that I haven't said to lovers. Maybe it's not strange that afterwards I really did feel like we'd been intimate, since revealing oneself is much more powerful than processing someone else's stuff, emotional or physical. And he, of course, wanted to do this again. He said, maybe we can meet, in Central Park, and "you won't be disappointed." Yikes. I hesitated, indicating that we need to find out whether there's any chance that we're actually compatible in an anonymous atmosphere first. But we did exchange first names, and I am curious and might want to meet him if this goes on. I hope it does. Imagine having a regular lover whom you've never met. Wowsa.

If I sent you an article of clothing, would it be stolen? I just have it in my head that you need an oversized cotton shirt the color of yellow mud that they're selling at the Gap. It's so Out of Africa. But would you ever get it? Are things settling down there? Did you run outside in the rain and pretend you were taking a shower? Maybe you should just come home. Or else, stay, and you'll be here soon enough, I'm convinced. Either way you'll be stranger and wiser, like Dorothy. Did anyone tell you that it snowed here these past couple days? It's Easter and it's snowing. Okay, it's 11:15. Bedtime. I just ate a lot of Hershey's Hugs and I feel really sick. I need to get it together. I'm angry this time.

Love,

H

P.S. But oh, how I cherish my little home!

April 20

Hilary—

Guess what: Because the water is so bad, Peace Corps is pulling us out of Ramisi. Hold all mail. In two weeks, when they can find us a new school, new town, and new house, we will leave.

On this island where we are currently having a deeply pleasant vacation, the only power is donkey—I have a new deeper understanding of what it means to be a beast of burden and I'll never be yours. It entails continually getting the crap beaten out of you while carrying heavy things. And you don't have arms. I like arms.

More when we get back to Ramisi.

Love,

K8

Dear Hilary,

Yesterday I sent you a postcard and today I got a letter from you saying that yesterday you sent me a postcard and today you are sending me a letter and today I am sending you a letter, "if you're getting me," as they say around here. We're in sync even this far away :-) (Do I have to make my smiley man sideways even when I'm writing by hand?)

I am really glad that the cybersex guy wasn't your brother because I think I would've had to go into therapy too if it had been. Isn't everything you type on your computer recorded somewhere and isn't that scary? I couldn't even do stuff like that on paper I could burn. Even if it were all lies. But I'm glad you can and I think you should keep it up because I want more stories. And tell me about your very own apartment. Will you draw it for me?

On our vacation we traveled far to a shallow but huge lake. It was a solidly brown color from mud, and the sun made it yellowy. It was also raining, so there was a twilight kind of light illuminating it, and there were silhouettes of mountains in the background. The shore, before the rise to the hills, was a wide-open, muddy plain where there were humpy cows and pure white fairy-tale cranes. In the middle of this flat lake in a small boat, we turned to see a small and harmless tornado of dust start in the town. Like it was Kansas. Then in a minute there were thirty of them. In the other direction a huge black storm cloud was darkening a rocky island. A hippo and its little hippo baby surfaced and ambled toward the boat. A double rainbow appeared over our shoulders. A fisherman in a boat made of straw, wearing very little, paddled over to us to give us a fish. The driver of our boat took the fish and, as it flopped, shoved some wood in it to make it float. Then he called the eagles, and they swooped down for it. A crocodile came out of the brush and submerged, and we waited out the rain on the rocky island under some thatching with some chatting children. And that was only day one of the trip.

Right now we're in the staff room in Ramisi on the first day of the new term—still very few students, no surprise. As I told you, yes, we're going to a new site next week. At first, as we walked to our house from the road, coming back from our trip, we thought, Oh Ramisi, how can we leave when we've come so far here! When we're starting to know how things go? How can we make friends all over again? But within hours, I started to feel sick again—you have to drink a lot of the water because it's so hot here all the time. Then, school reopened, with the headmaster caning the only students here and making them kneel in the brutal sun for an hour for not speaking to him with the proper respect. While we were on vacation another Peace Corps volunteer told us that a teacher at his school hit a student on her head with a chalkboard eraser until she got a bloody nose, so it's not just our school. We won't be sorry to leave here; we only hope that we're not jumping out of the frying pan into the fire.

LOVE,
Kate

May 14

Dear Hilary,

We are leaving behind all our students and all our
friends to start again. I realized that for the four
months we lived in that very small village there
were nineteen funerals because of AIDS, malaria,
and diarrhea. On our last day in Ramisi, the hour
before we left, a slow and sad procession of
everyone in the village buried Mama Abdu's son in
our backyard. I feel miserable because we're leaving
and miserable because we don't want to stay.
Ramisi is a thoroughly unhealthy place, and the
town and all the people in it, some of whom are
now our friends, are dying. Kiss your family for
me, Hilary, because I wish I could kiss mine.

Love,
Kate

Part Three

May–October

Dear Kate,

Welcome to your new digs. I wanted this to be there to greet
you and to prove that I'm adaptable. I'm relieved that you've left
Ramisi for good. It was clearly taking its toll on your spirit, not
to mention your bodily health. My travails are of the, well,
American stock. It's Monday and I'm at home, waiting for a
bookshelf to be delivered. Also, I'm eating caramels and they
keep getting stuck in my teeth. Bear with me.

The happy news here is that my brother and Emily are finally
officially engaged. Steven and I talked about where he should
do it. Many times. He talked to my mother about it. He
probably talked to all his friends about it. But my suggestion
won. After much collaborative planning, Steven told her that
they were having dinner with me and my mother at a restaurant
down near the waterfront. Instead, out by the water, he gave
her the ring that they picked out together. While they were
having dinner I got dozens of white flowers and put them all
over their apartment to await their happy return. I never
expected to be part of this particular moment, but it gave me
the same kind of joy as being the sole witness at your marriage.
That "I'm a very important third wheel" feeling. I'm not a big
fan of diamonds, but in all the pictures from that evening (leave
it to Steven to bring a camera), Emily's ring is shining like a

Christmas tree light. It looks like a good omen, that ring glowing neon green as if their collective happiness were radiating from it. If it isn't clear already, the lady said yes. Now I get to hear Emily gushing about how cute Steven is whenever he farts until the end of time.

I'm afraid I have to fill you in on the hasty abort of my cyberaffair. Are you sitting down? A few days after my online encounter a chocolate bunny was anonymously dropped off at my Soho office. The receptionist's (totally lame) description of the guy who wouldn't leave his name led me and a few key work friends to believe that it had to be the cyberlover. Who else would do it? I was being stalked. As I'd thought, anyone my age in NYC with a media job and a penchant for black clothes would have only to ask five of his closest friends if they knew a Hilary and one would certainly say, "Hilary who works at P——?" and the jig would be up. So I was all worked up about that for twenty-four hours until Stack called back and said he was the Easter bunny. False alarm.

Then Sunday KingX emailed me saying, "Hey, remember me? Contact me soon, we'll chat." Now, I don't want to get too technical here, but when someone sends you an email you get to see his or her name as it has been registered in the system. Through some detailed sleuthing not worth your time (though very Sherlock Holmesian on my part), it became clear to me that it was very likely this guy was someone who works with me. Someone (Lord help me!) whom I know slightly. I cross-checked the ID of KingX and the ID of my colleague and, yes, it was a match, without a doubt. Now, maybe I shouldn't have checked, but once I even suspected I just had to. I guess I violated the privacy of cyberculture. But, regardless, I discovered that I work with the guy with whom I'd exchanged words that you just don't use with people you ever expect to meet in person, particularly in an office environment.

Oh, the embarrassment. So much for anonymity. So much for the continuing drama of a cyberaffair. So much for my job. I was so horrified when I figured it out that I shut my office door and put my head down on my desk, red and giggling. I alternated between that position and pacing the three-foot floor space in my windowless office. Being me, as I like to say, is a full-time job. I was positive that if he hadn't figured it out already, he soon would. He would see me in the cafeteria and a terrible and true realization would settle over him with all the reality of, of, let's see—the overhead lighting of a swimwear dressing room? An ex-lover's journal? A ton of bricks? In retrospect, this seems a little less likely, but I was convinced that I had to clear the air. So I returned his email, writing, "Turns out I was right—we do sort of know each other. We work for the same company. I'm not saying what we did was wrong, but it's pretty embarrassing under the circumstances. When you recover from this news, tell me something to relieve the humiliation." That was Monday. By Wednesday I'm thinking that he (a) hasn't gotten the email, (b) hasn't recovered, (c) thinks I'm unattractive, or (d) is just plain chicken, but I have not heard back from him. And it turns out that I want some kind of response. I know what you're wondering. Is he my type? The best answer I can give is that I wouldn't pick him out of a crowd. (Oh and yes, of course, he lied to me online about what his job is and how tall he is, and lied when I asked him if he had lied about anything. All's fair in the world of cyberfantasy, but did I lie? What do you think?) So eventually I did hear back from him, something decent about how we'll keep it our little secret.

Now we just see each other in the halls at work. Were we a cybermatch? Definitely. But are we a match in reality? We are both too shy and awkward to find out. How do you talk to someone when you've had sex with him without ever speaking? And you thought that if you did meet it would be eventual, and carefully negotiated? Next to this a one-night stand is Jiffy Pop. Awkwardness aside, it's clear to me that I had hoped for something real, not from him the guy I work with, but from Mystery Guy KingX. I was curious about a virtual affair, but I realized that what I truly wanted was for it to lead to a real affair, with a three-dimensional person.

The only multidimensional person I like lately is Josh Stack, and everybody likes Josh Stack. I'm not saying I *like* like him or that "everybody" *like* likes him, but he's such an excellent boyfriend substitute. For example, yesterday we ate cold borscht and then walked around a little community garden in the middle of the city. We headed to his apartment, where he fed me watermelon and kiwi and a chocolate bunny that was left over from Easter (envious yet?), but in spite of all that I don't think he will ever be my real-life boyfriend, which both makes me sad and doesn't. Maybe I don't want him, but I want him to want me. Are you beginning to grasp the ambivalence here? Also, in the three-dimensional category, I must confess that I lapsed and had sex with Jason on the floor of my new apartment, but it was an accident, I swear. I tripped and fell on him. And then I thought, Kate forbade me to do that. You won't see or hear his name again. I am resolute.

Now that you know a little about the floor of my apartment, I'll fill you in on some of the less stimulating details. There's a communal roof, and we're one of the tallest buildings around. It's like being on a big ship sailing up Seventh Avenue. The building has a doorman, which is a luxury that I never considered before, but the effect is that I feel utterly safe. It has made me realize that in every other place I've lived in the city, I've visualized an assailant breaking in through the fire escape and attacking me in my sleep. I wasn't even being paranoid, just practical. But now there's no fire escape and no dark hallways. I face east. Well, I turn a bit, but the windows in the apartment face east. There are some water towers on the roofs out there, and I look at them as I eat cereal on my new, used steel table. Otherwise, I have very little furniture, but I'm so rarely home that all I really need is the bed. Steven made me a new bed, which is a prize. It's built of plumbing pipes, and I attached faucets to the two pipes at the head so the bed looks like a big sink and I don't have to get up to have a drink. Bet you don't get that in old Kenya. Choosing furniture is a new, albeit underwhelming, act of self-definition. I like nice, warm bottle greens, with enough metal stuff that no one messes with me.

Unfortunately, it didn't take me long to discover that there is a horse-footed woman living upstairs from me, disturbing the peace. She trots back and forth across my ceiling from early in the morning until late at night, dragging heavy furniture across the floor. Just my luck. Still, even this constant interruption can't shatter my joy at finally living alone for the first time ever. I'm already talking to myself and developing unsociable habits. I do the crossword in the morning with my spoon and pen skillfully held in one hand. I sleep in the buff. I sing too loudly and shower in the dark. No one knows.

I totally-otally miss you. The end of this letter was supposed to be all about you, but now I've taken so long talking about me that I don't really have room for you. But I'm thinking about you. (I got that from my most Hallmark friend, but isn't it a nice thing to say? And it's true.) I want to know how Dave is, please (other than a fearsome snake-killer). Finally, Saturday I went to a party and there was a woman there named Hilary who was wearing exactly the same outfit as I. Life's little miracles . . . of which you are one, so take care of yourself and watch out for cobras, okay?

But now let me face today,

H

Hi Hilary,

We've arrived (as had your letter, thank you). Everything here is better than in Ramisi. The land is lush and productive, there's more food and cleaner water, and the people are healthier. Neighbors are constantly at our door saying *"Hodi!"* (meaning something like "I'm about to come in") and sitting down for a friendly chat. Our house is made of carefully packed mud with a thatched roof and cement floors. We have wooden carved Swahili doors—real art. The bedroom and a sitting room are under the thatching, along with the *choo* and a storage room, and we'll cook in the open courtyard. What makes this house wonderful already is that the cement floor extends out past the front wall making a sort-of porch. It's perfect for neighborhood children to play on with their homemade wire cars, balls of knotted up plastic bags, and rolling tire rims, and we've made bunches of small friends already. Right now, David is sharing pencils and drawing goats and *matatus* with Uba, a precocious and constantly dirty three-year-old, and her slightly older brother Sefu, who always has a serious expression on his face.

Yesterday morning we were walking around our new hometown admiring all the lush banana trees, led by one of Dave's new students, Hamadi. (The land here, especially when there's a full moon, looks exactly like *Where the Wild Things Are* but without the Wild Things. Maybe Dave could gnash and roll.) Anyway, Hamadi pointed to a gray rocklike thing that I could just make out up ahead. "See that rock?" he asked. "That's an elephant." Needless to say, we ran. On the way home, he showed us several palm trees that had been pulled out of the ground the way we would pull up a dandelion. I noticed that elephant footprints are much bigger when you aren't sure where the elephant is.

Things are wet hereabouts, it still being the very, very rainy season and all, and living under thatching can be a little moldy, if you can imagine. Although the world is sprouting in a very pleasing way, when our clothes sprout, and we can't dry them, it is less pleasing. This morning I went to wash up our plastic dishes and thought to myself, I don't remember leaving bananas out all over them. Then I realized that they weren't bananas after all. They were rather large, greasy, yellowish slugs. If that doesn't give you a nightmare, I give up.

We're settling in well. I nailed a bunch of nails into the workbench that's in our kitchen courtyard. Now we have a place to put the rags (so we don't burn our hands taking pots of boiling water off the fire) and the scoop (that we use to get water out of the big storage vat) and the plastic strainer (through which we pour most liquids to get rid of the bugs, sticks, and dead ants that invariably fall in). That should help the bumbling-around-in-the-dark-trying-to-make-dinner-but-can't-find-the-candles type of problem.

Our new neighbor Mwanamisi (mother of Uba and Sefu and

three other, older children) came over last night to show me how to make coconut rice, *wali wa nazi*. Kate, you say, but you already know how to make coconut rice! Yes, I say, but I don't know how to make friends. So David and I were rushing around trying to make reality match what we realized we had probably said in Kiswahili ("I think I said we'd 'already' cleaned the rice and we 'were doing' laundry."). Mwanamisi arrived midway through the coconut-milk-making process and was chatting with us about how to cook it really well, soft and sweet. As far as I could tell, she was complimenting me on what I had done so far, except there was one little part that I didn't catch, and her tone was less spunky, so I figured I probably didn't put enough salt in or something. But, all in all, I was pretty excited at not being totally incompetent at cooking. Later I checked on that verb to figure out what I'd done wrong. Here's what my dictionary said about it. (I mean, I just *"haribu"*ed it—how bad could it be, right?) *"kuharibu:* v. injure, destroy, spoil, damage, ruin, demoralize, spoil work, break up an expedition, devastate a country, cause miscarriage, pervert, corrupt." That's what I did to the rice. Good thing we like potatoes, eh?

Last week we had lunch at the house of another new neighbor, Rama. After the meal, he said that he was very happy that we could be friends, he had thought that Americans didn't like Muslims. Then he asked about my religion. Now often, I've hedged about God, because everyone here seems to be very religious, and I've wanted to be accepted. I'd let people believe what they wanted about my God-feelings. But this guy had been criticizing his wife (who wasn't eating with us) and backhanding his kids throughout the whole meal, so I was ready to risk his rejection. I said that I was glad we could be friends too, even though I'm not religious. He was very quiet. "You worship the devil?" he asked. I talked about believing in goodness and in trying to help others, but when I finished, he summed up by saying, "If you are not with God, you are against Him." He then drew a line on the ground with his finger. "It is simple, you just choose, this side with God, or this side with Satan." I said for me it wasn't like that. He shook his head and has carefully avoided me ever since. (He has come to the house occasionally to borrow our hammer, though. I sort of want to tell him it's Satan's hammer.)

We do still have a bit of a water problem (i.e., the pipe that leads to a spigot close to the village is only turned on for several hours each day, if at all), but when we do get some, it's clean. So, since it hasn't been on for several days and we didn't get very much last time, I'm feeling a bit grungy. And you know me and my passion for hot showers.

We've only just started teaching, Dave at a school of only sixty boys and girls a ways up the path, and me at a huge school of about 900 boys, a ways down the path. It's hard to tell yet how the two will compare with Ramisi Secondary. They do seem better so far. We're about to go to a *harambee* at Dave's school—basically a live telethon only you just give money and don't get an umbrella with a logo. Everyone sits outside on chairs facing a big table and watches everybody else give money, a shilling at a time. A big donation gets three simultaneous claps. It's very communal, though it takes forever.

I'm so happy for you that Steven is engaged. "Sister Emily" has a nice ring to it. Say hi to your cyberboy for me.

Yours always,
Kate

Dear K8,

There is a sound in my apartment of air being released. I'm a little afraid. Otherwise I'm having a peaceful interlude. I don't have a TV and don't plan to get one. My plants are doing well. In fact, I have such a green thumb that a sponge in my kitchen is sprouting like a Chia Pet. I'm serious. It's very dada. I'm having a glass of ruby red grapefruit juice, struggling to like it. My mother graciously informed me that my daily orange juice is "high in sugar." I'm trying to think of grapefruit juice like broccoli rabe or Campari, where you embrace the bitterness. If I drink it every day I will come to like it, I believe. Sort of like having a day job.

Speaking of which, I'm officially on a job safari. I know I haven't been at this company long enough, but there's a new owner and a "reorg" every week and I can't see when things will straighten out. People at work have been teasing me about needing to go to Attitude Camp. You know how grumpy I act sometimes, just to keep everyone on their toes. But now whenever I try to be cheerful they think it's a joke. It has dawned on me that I am finally too old to be a prodigy. There is some relief in this, but it also takes its toll on my ambition. Sure, I want success in my field. I want to be respected for my ideas and to earn the freedom to choose my projects. But since

I apparently won't be the first or best at anything, it's hard to know how fast to go. Still, right now I'm pretty eager to move and so am open to many jobs of the online and editorial ilk.

As for me and the cybersex guy, we literally haven't spoken since we acknowledged by email that the jig was up. I mean, I see him almost every day at work, or on the train to work, and we don't look at each other. I think it's silly, and I know I should just say something, but there are always crowds of people around. My latest idea is that I'll tap him on the shoulder persistently saying, Excuse me (tap, tap), we had cybersex, excuse me.

Delia just called. Oh, is it worth explaining? I've been kind of annoyed at Delia lately because she only, literally and astoundingly, only ever calls me when she wants something from me. I called her to send her an invitation to my party and she never called back, so I never invited her. But then, when she heard I was having a party, she went ahead and invited herself. Now, turns out, Stack got her number at the party and asked her out. It felt like a double betrayal. How did I find this out? Oh, because she just called me for Stack's number. I thought for an instant that she was calling to say hi, but then, like magic, the reason emerged. Stack clearly isn't gay, although I appreciate your confidence that someone who didn't fall for me would have to be gay. Note: Stack specifically did not tell me he'd gotten Delia's phone number and had decided to call her. How could he after what I had told him about her questionable behavior toward me?

I don't know why I'm surprised. This is exactly the way the world is. By believing that this level of loyalty was possible I have only furthered my chances at being disappointed in my friends. I'm embarrassed to be upset by this. I think I'm holding them to standards to which they are oblivious. I can't believe I'm feeling possessive and competitive about my friends. Petty, right? I guess maybe I had more hope that Stack would like me than I knew. Or maybe it's that I'm not involved in my work, only in finding new work. But also I don't get what the model for friendship is in this time of life. Look at me—right now I'm trying to imagine why Delia and Stack won't work out. Now my own behavior isn't meeting my friendship standards. This whole thing makes me want to retreat, to stick to you, Steven, Emily, and a few other people I know I can trust to the South Pole and back. The hard part is that I think of Delia and Stack as falling into that category. It's okay, it's okay. There are good things in the air. (But, God, I'm still angry!)

Spring is here, and Steven brought me to a sedate barbecue full of kind strangers last weekend on the Upper West Side. Two excellent doctors whom I met a year ago showed up and were talking like doctors. For example, Larissa was eating a hamburger and she said, "It's funny that I'm eating this because I'm a vegetarian. (pause) My bone marrow is like, 'Yes!'" They were talking about examining the rich and famous. The way they expressed this was by saying, "I did Nixon." There were two doctors at the barbecue who had "done" Nixon, and Larissa had "done" Jackie O. A rectal exam to be specific.

Larissa will be my new friend, I hope. She wants to set me up with her friend William Strong. That's Dr. Strong to you and me.

I'm ready for an introduction because yesterday I got my hair cut by April. She works in the Chelsea Hotel, alongside the ghosts of Dylan Thomas, Thomas Wolfe and others. Hers is one of those intimidating salons where I feel like an inferior, if not unwelcome, client because my modeling career isn't moving fast enough and because there are always supercool, grungy but coifed people hanging around and pushing out onto the window balconies for a cigarette or five. April cuts like Edward Scissorhands, shears and hair flying. I close my eyes and hope. This time she stood me up and, without warning, attacked my eyebrows with tweezers. I was powerless to interfere. She is an artist. I have been repaired.

I'm glad you have a new friend, even if she doesn't appreciate your cooking. You can have me over for coconut rice anytime. How about that husband of yours? Does it work for you to socialize together, or does he ditch you to go out drinking with the men? Can you hold hands in public? (Do you anyway? Turns out I can't picture it.)

One more thing. I summoned up all my courage to go talk nicely to my upstairs neighbor yesterday, to tell her that I hear every step she takes and every piece of furniture she moves, and she was sorry for being noisy and I was sorry the building is the way it is and still she woke me up this morning at six, apparently rearranging her living room. If she wanted wall-to-wall carpeting I would weave it for her. Yes, this is what I will do for love. I'm in love with a good night's sleep. When I bought my apartment, with my last dime, I thought I was buying a life alone. I never thought my upstairs neighbor would turn out to be a bakery chef, requiring that she rise ("to make the donuts," as she laughingly said. Ha ha ha.) at four in the morning.

> *Lots of rest, care, affection, sympathy, empathy,*
> *goodwill, respect, loyalty, hugs and kisses,*
>
> H

P.S. It took me a few days to finish this and now that sponge is dead.

Dear Hil,

You are very small and cute and un-fuzzy, which you reminded me by writing.

I'm in the new staff room right now, between classes, and I just want to let you know that I still will never fit in fashion-wise. Yes, I wear my slip and skirt, but I can't seem to ever keep them in good repair or to get them as clean as my colleagues do. These other women also tend to wear secondhand American prom dresses or gorgeous, brightly patterned African print tops and skirts. My sallow complexion can't really carry it off, and I usually feel quite frumpy in my cotton tee shirts and long skirts. Just so you know I haven't changed. The male teachers here at the school are very seventies-hip. I mean, Afros, tight tight bum-hugging dress pants, plasticky leather belts, often jewel-studded, with long-collared shirts and wide brown stripes with orange ties. They would probably be very into you in your new haircut.

The staff room itself is amazing at the moment, even to me, and I consider myself somewhat used to things (having now lived here nine months already!). The next-door toilet (which, I'm told, has never worked) is overflowing into here, so there's a quarter inch of, shall we say, not crystal clean water all over the floor. Teachers ate lunch in here yesterday, so there are bits of rice on all the rickety tables. Papers are scattered around and floating on the floor. The walls are filthy, having last been painted before Christ. Cockroaches crawl across the shelves, eating the rice and exploring the yellowed, gritty stacks of papers. The windows are mostly cracked with holes, and there are ripped and filthy curtains with a pattern of black and green flowers. Droppings and pieces of sand coat everything, making visible the vast expanses of cobwebs and spiders in every corner. The chairs are wobbly or have broken backs. The few books are tattered and look like they were printed a really long time ago. In a few minutes we'll all drink hot sugar water and I'll listen to talk about how dumb the students are and who should've gotten caned this morning. Yes, the school situation is still quite bad.

Another problem is that Kwale Secondary School stinks. Literally. There aren't any toilets other than the broken teacher-toilet, and there aren't any usable *choos* either. We all use the woods. Dave and I estimated how much urine (not to mention anything else) gets dumped in the grounds around the classrooms and dorms daily: 200 gallons. So you can imagine how it smells. (Only, as you can imagine, urine isn't the predominant smell.) The headmaster told the boys to walk farther away from the school when they go, "or else we will have an outbreaking of one of those funny-funny diseases." It's nasty.

As for Dave, he's pretty much doing how I'm doing. He teaches in two schools. In the morning he teaches at one, and then, because he has afternoons free, he joins me to teach at this school also. It means he has a lot of biking to do. This was a problem during the rains because the bike would have benefited from skis, and he needed to change clothes after riding because of the red mud that coated him from head to toe. But it's okay now because the rains are over and the mud has dried out. The students love him to death, and when he got to the soccer field yesterday to watch their game they started cheering and yelling, *"Mwalimu, Mwalimu!"* (Teacher!) It was very cute. He'd told them he was going to "take a snap," about which they were very excited. They were asking when he was going to take it and he said, "No, no, I said I would take you a snack! Here, I brought you some *sukuma wiki* (spinach)." They were totally confused but laughed when he took out the camera. You know, foreign-language jokes. He's also the bug killer of the two of us. I pretty much avoid killing anything even if it's poisonous and I really should. On the other hand, I'm the one who usually makes the *chapati,* which is not logical because his are better than mine. I suspect he resists cooking them because it pains him to put in as much fat as they need to make them tasty and crisp.

Yesterday I noticed he had a huge blister on his finger so I, naturally, asked him what happened. He kind of mumbled and hedged a little and then finally explained that when he had finished flossing his teeth he had sat there with the dental floss without knowing what to do with it. He figured he might as well burn it. While holding it. As it turns out, African dental floss is explosive, so, even though he promptly dropped it (and the lighter, which shattered into a billion pieces as I later discovered in my bare feet), he still burned the hell out of his finger. Men.

Meanwhile, a few days ago I managed to splatter some hot fat on my legs while overexuberantly flipping a frying *chapati*. I got some small but ugly burns on my legs. Mwanamisi saw them and told me the best thing to do was to put the medicine Colgate on them. I hope for her sake that toothpaste kills bacteria or something, since I'm sure she does that for herself and her kids.

When we're not trying to take teaching up to the level where we don't want to kill ourselves and our students to put us out of our misery, we are having a great time here. The latest episode was being ushered into a tiny mud house decorated with millions of bits of colored rags tied from wires (like the colored triangles at a car dealer) for a welcome dance. Women tied *kangas* (sarilike cloths) around their butts to hang down like tails and shook their booties to the drumbeats. Yes, I tried to dance, but I couldn't wiggle my patootie nearly quickly enough or long enough to consider it really dancing. The women were laughing and trying to push my rump back and forth appropriately. Meanwhile, the men were watching and drinking alcoholic home brew. (I confess to sneaking an unwomanly sip or two.) The cutest little girl in the world and an old woman with rotten teeth and a bald head did the Dance of the Butterfly together.

Do you get that I still don't know what you actually *do* at work? Will I still be your friend even if I call you because I want something?

> *Still love,*
> *Kate*

P.S. Hi there Hilary. Kate really liked the *mbangara*. She is trying to convince me that she has malaria. I think it's just because she doesn't know how to say "hangover" in Kiswahili.

> *Dave*

KWALE

June 28

Dear Hil,

You know how I said that Kwale is better than Ramisi? Well,
not in the schools. Dave is getting gray hairs. (Keep in mind
people all over Kenya consider Kwale High to be one of the
best schools in the Coast Province.) Today, an ordinary day, the
headmaster gave his morning speech with the usual humdingers
in it. He challenged the students to name the worst sin it is
possible to commit. Answer: disobeying a rule. Then he told
them that if they hadn't paid their school fees, they had to go
home. And, well, "the rest of you dunderheads can go to hell."
(Afterwards, one teacher asked me what a "dunderhead" was.
When I told him, he said, "But hell is only for sinners, and
people who aren't very smart can still follow the Lord, can't
they?" For the record, I said I thought so.)

Then, as I sat in the staff room, the Teacher on Duty brought
in students, one by one. They get beaten for getting low scores
on their exams. The form one students (some are only thirteen)
were terrified, cowering, even in tears. If they score very low,
they get four whacks of the cane. If they flinch, they get an
extra whack, so they always grip the chairs in front of them as
they bend over. The T.O.D. took off his watch ("So I won't
break it"), rolled up his sleeves, and stretched. He got a firm
grip, took a few practice strokes, and then he started whipping

the boys. Meanwhile, the other teachers were jeering and laughing at each child, and if it was a student they didn't like they would yell, "Give him five! Give him five!" One student came back afterwards because his beating was so brutal that he thought he might need to see a doctor. The T.O.D. looked at the gashes on his back and decided he was right but instructed him harshly to say another student did it to him. I always leave when this kind of thing is going on. The first few times I saw it, or even heard it, it would make my palms sweat and my heart pound, and now it only makes me feel sick. It is deeply disturbing to me that I seem to be capable of getting even a little bit used to it. I don't want to get even a little bit used to it.

The assistant headmaster told me what the teachers in Ramisi told us, "This is the only way we Africans can learn." The other teachers agree. They said even if the students in my classes learn without caning and without verbal slashing, it's because I'm different as an American, and because there is the atmosphere of "discipline" on the school compound despite me. Since parents treat children this way, they explain, teachers must continue with the same severity. (It is true that parents ask teachers to cane their children, and are often more severe with them than teachers are.) It's a never-ending discussion in the staff room, fueled on their side by the images of American schools full of weapons, violence, and disrespect for authority. Although Dave and I are on friendly terms with the other teachers, and we often exchange visits and share meals and tea with each other, on a deeper level we are alienated from them, and they from us.

Yesterday, when we were in the Peace Corps Office getting booster shots, we ran into another volunteer who's been here some time and had dinner with him. He seems to have thoroughly assimilated. His Kiswahili is excellent, he is very close to several Kenyans and knows an incredible amount about Kenyan culture. As do his colleagues, he's going to nightclubs and sleeping with prostitutes. He now beats his students with a cane. He said he feels as though he's "floating in limbo." I think the feeling might be from tearing away from the rules he had for himself in the States and from the strangeness of following only those rules the people around you follow. I had thought I wanted to be the kind of person who really "embraces" a culture. Now I don't think so. I now know, for example, that I'm not interested in exploring whether or not brutality improves education, or whether or not subservience in women improves marriages. On these topics, my mind is not open.

One of my students, named Baya (which means "bad"), is small, probably around twelve, and exceedingly cute. Once he brought me a story he'd written for fun entitled "About My Favorite Animal Chicken." Anyway, two days ago he went to the Teacher on Duty because he was feeling sick and wanted to go to the hospital. The teacher thought he was faking and sent him back to class. Then yesterday people noticed he was missing. Those questioned had last seen him laughing and crying, running around and curled in a fetal position. We learned today that he probably has cerebral malaria, which either kills you or leaves you with permanent brain damage when you don't catch it right away. I'm waiting for news of him.

To feel better, after school I'm going home to play with my David and our neighborhood children. The other day Rehema, the mother of one of the children, ended her visit to us by asking, "You give children time? Your time? That is interesting, we don't do that here." She was especially interested that David, a man, would spend time playing with children. It was hard for me to tell if she thought we were extravagant and foolish or if she thought it was a good idea. The next time her son came over to play, he brought us some coconut cassava in a fancy plastic dish, from her. Decode that, if you can.

Love,
Kate

Dear Katey,

My boss is out of the office; I've run out of job leads to pursue
for the day; and I don't have a ton to do. So here's the whole
skinny on my blind date with William Strong, that you may
experience the exhaustive detail of our fumblings as we wend
our way toward inevitable redundancy, if not failure.

I actually had two blind dates this weekend. The first was on
Saturday, and before it I went to yoga, taught by my friend
Tatiana from high school. I told her, I've got this blind date
tonight, and suddenly I can't remember what people talk about.
She disappeared behind incense and mirrors and returned with
a book called *The Rules: Time-Tested Secrets for Capturing the Heart
of Mr. Right*. It was very funny. Also, I learned a lot from it. Now
I know how to behave on dates one through three in order to
entrance an unwitting man and trap him into marriage. Lovely
and useful, huh? Well, it slept its way to the top of the slew of
scary dating advice books. The *Rules* are stuff like: Present
yourself as nice but busy. Don't worry about keeping the
conversation going. Don't ever call him. Basically it's for
women who don't have lives, so they can behave as though they
do until a man is smitten, at which point the illusion they've
created will conveniently give way to the business of planning a
wedding. My mother, unfortunately, has also gotten her hands

on this book. It's not like she's dying for me to hunt down a husband, but there are rules she still wants me to follow. Like being "a nice girl," not fooling around on the first date, letting him pay. Whatever. Among my many complaints about the book—the virtues of which are being overdebated in various media—is that it's hard enough trying to be original already. What I don't need is a best-seller that tells me and a million other presumably diverse people exactly how to be "spontaneous," how to be "a creature unlike any other."

I'm going to cut to Dr. Strong, the second and more interesting date of the weekend. I waited to meet him on Sunday, coddling my collection of hope and despair, tasting the last of the Power Bar that was supposed to keep me awake through the ordeal. There he came, slightly late, loping diagonally across the street toward Ciel Rouge, a tiny, all-red bar with a gold, baroque-y tent in the back. As he approached, blind date number whatever, I saw immediately that we would actually consider each other. He didn't have any nervousness or urge to win me. I mean, it was obvious that he didn't dress up for the night. But he trudged toward me with a step that seemed somehow familiar. And he had a dark beard, which I thought was worth a try. We ordered mint juleps under the tent behind Ciel Rouge. Our conversation was easy, as if we'd been reading the same books for years. Except he's ahead of me. This, coupled with his sense of humor, which I can't describe, is part of what makes him a contender. I like his voice—his sentences come slowly, looking both ways before crossing.

Over our second round of drinks he confessed that he was drunker than he thought he should be. He followed this by stating that he didn't think arranged marriages were such a bad thing, but for this day and age he would update the tradition by allowing a person to choose his or her own matchmaker. He said that he would choose Larissa, the woman who set us up. Ignoring all premature insinuations here, my response was that I would choose you as my matchmaker (even though your only attempt was years ago and landed me with poor Albert, and you did that entirely for your own amusement). Then William, having essentially declared our potential, picked up my hand to study my nails. I, of course, couldn't bear to have him think that I'm the kind of career girl who has regularly polished nails. No, I had to explain that I'd had an interview at Condé Nast, where fashion is everything, and that when I got to the threshold fifteen minutes before the interview I realized that I couldn't go through the doors without a manicure. But I digress. Walking me home from our refined two drinks apiece, he slid an arm around my waist, and I didn't know what to do. It was certainly too soon to talk about it—too early and embarrassing to say: "Um, excuse me but I don't think we know each other enough for you to do what you are doing with your arm." Various means of escape: tying a shoelace, doing a pirouette, even detaching the arm and holding the hand for a brief instant before dropping it, all seemed to send the wrong message. That hand around my waist, it was sending the right message.

We went up to my roof, where it was a perfect temperature. It was the exact temperature that, on other excursions to my roof, has made me yearn for boy-company. You know how in the right setting with the right weather one can't help but feel vigorous. My roof makes me want to sing. Lucky for us all, I refrained. We looked down at Seventh Avenue and William observed that all the cars were coming downtown, toward us, which meant that their lights were white, not red, and that from our angle we couldn't see the traffic lights. How long have I lived here and not realized that Seventh Avenue was a river of white lights? So in a moment when I was nearly overwhelmed by where his hands were and where they might choose to go from there, I was reminded that he might be, well, a very interesting person.

We were two interesting people who barely knew each other, facing one another in an awkward half hug. I was thinking how odd it was and wondering when he would try to kiss me and what I would do then when it turned out that we were already kissing, and that of the options I had, stopping wasn't the one I'd take. In Act I, scene i, of the kiss a single sentence ran through my head: "This man is thirty-five." Eight extra years he'd been alive and kissing. So long, ex-boyfriends, I thought, the way an astronaut thinks, So long, Earth. I'm going with thirty-five. After he left, I went back to my apartment, closed the door, and fell back against it, hands clasped, eyes heavenward, like a sitcom girl.

But this was Sunday, and now it's Wednesday, and not only is it harder to remember what he was like but I'm not even sure I would recognize him out of context on the street. We might be having dinner tonight and I'm kind of nervous.

I'm sorry that the conditions at this school are so intolerable. I support your closed-mindedness with the dedication of a flying buttress. And, for the record, you have never ever called me because you needed something, not even a phone number or a tissue. Make that a goal for when you're back. I have real doubts that you're protecting your skin sufficiently, but at least you will be able to say to your grandkids, "These wrinkles, little Hilary, are from the years I spent in Africa." Protect everything else also, will you please? I need you back in one piece, weathered or no.

That's all for now.

—H

NEW YORK CITY

July 12

Happy Birthday, Farthest Kate!

May this be the farthest birthday you ever have.
Today I'm sending you what I hope is a year's
supply of peanut butter cups and a new towel,
which is the closest thing to a clean, healthy
shower that I can imagine.

  Thanks for being born, and please continue to
be so.

Love,

H

Dear Hilary,

Remember the burns on my legs from cooking *chapati*? Well, of course they got infected (maybe I should have tried the toothpaste), and I ended up having to go to the doctor in Mombasa yesterday for some antibiotics. Fine, right? So I walk into the office and sit down and the doctor looks at the infections for a really long time. Then she looks up at me and says, "What's this?" Hoping she was testing me and not actually wondering, I explained that some of my small burns had gotten infected. She looked at them for another really long time and then asked, "You are in Peace Corps?" Thinking she might be stalling for time to figure out what to do, I tried to work in some hints about antibiotics while explaining my job here in Kenya. When there was dead silence after my explanation, I assumed the hints hadn't really taken hold. She looked at my wounds again and said to herself kind of wistfully, "I think you can't come here every day for new plasters. . . ." I sort of panicked at this point, imagining making the four-hour trip daily for her to put a Band-Aid on my gangrenous legs, so I asked her if maybe the other doctor I had gone to for my last infection had done the right thing by giving me antibiotics? Slightly offended, she asked me which antibiotic and proceeded to write me a prescription for the same one. Then she examined my legs again for a while, looked up at me, and said, "Maybe we should clean it?" I agreed and immediately regretted it when that seemed to really slow things down. Finally, she said, "But . . . how did you burn your legs if you are cooking with your hands?" I explained that the fat splattered when I flipped the *chapati*. Ah-ha! That really caught her interest. How could I flip *chapati* with a fork? I need to buy an instrument. Yes, an instrument. "It's about this long," she said, gesturing near her elbow, and it has a very flat end. Flat and square. Yes, this long, with a very flat end. Really I must get this instrument called a spa–tu–la. In fact, she drew me a picture of it and wrote the name of it in Hindi and Swahili so that I could get it from a clerk in a store. While the nurse was dressing my wounds, she came into the room again to make sure I had the concept. Really, she was very concerned. The nurse put an Ace bandage on my burns, and Dave and I left hurriedly to get the prescription filled before she could decide that we needed a whole dishes set. Don't you wish you could get pus-y blisters on your legs? Should I save some of my really big scabs for you? (And I know you want to point out that if we had registered for our wedding, we would already *have* a dish set.)

We're having problems at Dave's school with, get this, girls being possessed by *djinnis* (genies). Recently, the fiftieth girl fainted screaming with the whites of her eyes rolled down. Several have dropped out of school because of it. Some of them show up at our door in the evening to draw, and they look totally exhausted from screaming all day. Many of them have charms for protection now. Sefu has a ball of bits of colored string all knotted up and put on a string of palm leaf around his neck. Nazmin has a black leather thong around her upper arm with a little pouch of dried herbs in it. Nothing seems to be working yet, however. Zaina told me that it feels like a man is squeezing your neck when it happens to you, and you get hot. Mwanamisi says that some girls have been seeing a supernatural man with a *panga* who puts it to their throats and says he's going to slaughter them.

Here's the wisdom of the week from Dave: It's cool to see a zebra, but it's even cooler to be bored seeing a zebra. I'm happy for your new love—maybe.

Kate

Hey Kate,

Why, you ask, a handwritten letter from your cyberfriend?
Why indeed. Since you asked, it's because I am finally,
thankfully, between jobs (and therefore between computers)
again. My new job will be better because I'll be working for a
small, bookish website in the city. My career will have shape
again, thankfully. How relieved I was to commute for the last
time. The job doesn't start for another month, which gives me
time to play. One week has passed, and I spent it accomplishing
the tasks that work made impossible: painting my kitchen
mango; getting my dishwasher repaired; and repotting plants.
I'm afraid I'm becoming a less interesting person. I just painted
my toenails sky blue. See what I mean?

Do you remember August? There are only a few people left
in the city, and almost all of us spend as much time as possible at
the movies. Tonight Stack and I will go to the free movie in
Bryant Park behind the New York Public Library. They do this
all summer Mondays, showing classics on a huge screen
suspended, it seems, from the HBO building and other
midtown pinnacles. The park fills up with all kinds of people—
I think—I've only been once, to last season's finale, *The Sound of
Music.* It was incredibly surreal to see Julie Andrews spinning
across the mountainside surrounded by traffic and city lights.

Everyone sang along and hissed at the Nazis. Tonight is *The Wizard of Oz*. I wonder if people will go in costume.

Stack and I have been making Dreamsicles in the afternoons. They're just blended orange juice and vanilla frozen yogurt. Stack always tries to deviate from that recipe, with some new idea involving coffee ice cubes, so we can eventually make our fortune by publishing a frozen drink recipe book. I told him he's an idea-hamster. I never let him touch my Dreamsicle. Why change perfect? Did I mention that my apartment has ceiling fans in both rooms? They're working hard right now. It was my plan, this unemployed Monday morning, to go skate down the West Side Highway, but now I can't quite imagine upsetting my present comfort level. I'm not even a hundred percent positive that it's Monday, and I'd like to keep it that way.

Wedding plans for Steven and Emily proceed. Yesterday I went with Emily to check out her dress, which is just lovely: simple enough for Emily's tastes but transparent and architectural enough to suit Steven.

I'm a love story waiting to happen, don't you think? Sorry to hold back on you, but I've now been on several dates with Dr. Strong, and we are further contemplating each other. As part of that, we are using our lips and some other body parts. It's at a fragile, fragile point. I've been a little heady and addicted to his affection lately. How can I make it clear that I'm busy and hard to win (following *The Rules*) while on the exuberant vacation I have begun?

There's something sacred to this one, something that makes

me want to keep it between him and me and my journal, but (okay, okay, calm down) I suppose you deserve it, being so far away and all. So I will tell you this, and more. He stares and stares at me, and I can't hold his eyes. This past weekend we went hiking in the middle of New Jersey and came upon some trees that had long, thick vines hanging from many feet above. I grabbed one that looped down just above my head and hooked my feet over it, pulling myself up so I was sitting. William pushed me and there I was, swinging through the trees, about five feet above the ground. I thought, Who knew there was a jungle in New Jersey? Then we discovered a grove of pines planted so close together that there was no undergrowth, only a plush bed of pine needles. And a fine bed it made! The good news about public affection is that if you don't look at people they can't see you.

To further your vision of this love montage, you should know that we went camping together in the White Mountains of New Hampshire. Don't get me wrong. He's still something of a stranger, and I wasn't sure about going. But curled up in his tent by the light of a candle lantern, his arm around me as psychological shield against bears and other beasts, he made the suggestion that we sing camp songs. Camp songs! I looked at him incredulously, wondering, Where did you come from? Picture it: a little firefly of a tent huddled near a gurgling stream and a dying campfire, emitting a B-grade version of "The Circle Game." Another high school fantasy come true. Unreal. Now if only he'd carried my pack up the blasted mountain.

William is a *rara avis*. Let's see, he's deadpan; a self-described pervert (which so far means he reads Philip Roth and likes people better when they're unbathed); and he's so hairy that we were in a pharmacy and he was looking at the Rogaine and he said, "I have this area . . ." and he pointed to his knuckles, one of the few places on his body that aren't covered with nearly black hair. He may be unlike men I have liked in the past in that he holds a job and only plays guitar occasionally, but he shares, perhaps, a cynicism, and that deep, lazy voice with lovers past. He has insomnia in a very serious way. He goes to extremes to try to fall asleep. When we camped I'd wake up and find us head-to-toe.

When I'm with him, um, in layman's terms, it feels so right. But my ease is tempered by some hesitance, because while I find myself charmed by his oddities, I can tell he's discovering that I'm not Dream Girl, and I'm not sure how he'll react. Still, last night, like Scheherazade, he was allowed to stay until he guessed my middle name. When he was leaving I said, in an overly formal way, "I think I'm going to have to see you again," and he pulled me up to him and said, "You make me want to cry."

And you, Kate, you make me want to eat dinner, which I will now do.

—*H*

P.S. Did you ever receive your birthday package?

Dear Hilary,

You sent me a birthday package, did you? Are you sure you didn't mistakenly address it to "A Kenyan Postal Worker"?

Part 1: A Success Wish

In order to wish you success in your new job, I include a poem from an English language greeting card I bought in Mombasa:

> *As the moment to express your talent*
> *Continues to advance*
> *Equally your tantalizing wishes*
> *Continue to increase*
>
> *Fight like a wounded LION*
> *At-last let your gossip-wishers be filled with shame*
> *For in the end we shall discourse your victorious news*
> *With all the might.*

Part 2: Why There Is Chicken Blood on Our Steps and Holy Water Sprinkled on the Thatching of Our Roof

Because our house was haunted by *djinnis* and a witch doctor ceremonially exorcised it.

Part 3: On Something That Looks Like Dollhouse Rice but Isn't. At All.

My foot kind of hurt. It looked like an infected splinter was way deep inside it, so I got out the kitchen knife to do some operating. When I squeezed it, lots and lots of little tiny eggs came out along with a gooey membrane and the sac coating. Doesn't it seem like anyone who hasn't had an egg sac hasn't really been here? Did I tell you about Dave's? And how he fainted when they carved it out? In summary: It was gross. It hurt.

Okay, I've got a few questions about William. Does he appreciate your sense of humor? Does he like your poetry? Those would be good indicators. We're a little worried about the fact that he sleeps upside down, though, aren't we? In any case, it's clear that so far we like him. Camping is good. Singing is good. Why does he seem so old to me? Maybe it's because he's a doctor, and I'm still fucking around in Africa in my kneesocks (not really). (The kneesocks part.)

I am in a thorough state of confusion about my work life. Shouldn't I have led a nation or saved a camp of refugees or gotten the Nobel Prize for something by now? I am also in a thorough state of confusion about your work life. Will I have better luck getting you to tell me what you do at this new job? I lovingly picture you in front of a computer, typing. Right so far?

The idea of a whole new two-sided blank page is too much for me to handle right now, but I love you.

Kate

P.S.
Hi again another time, Hil.

Dave commented that Part 2 of my letter was kind of short. Which I know is true, but some things are so hard to explain. But I'll try.

For the last few months, the girls at Dave's school have been having problems with fits, as I think I've mentioned. They see a transparent, white-bearded man whispering that he's going to slit their throats with a *panga*. Upon seeing this, they go totally rigid, froth at the mouth, and scream incessantly and inconsolably for an hour or more. This sometimes happens with several dozen girls at once. It has become a common sight to see a row of students (in their uniform of red-checked shirts and purple skirts) carrying a girl across their arms who is stiff as a board and screaming hysterically.

Witch doctors have been coming off and on to do some ritual dances, rites, and chants, but nothing's been helping. By now, most of the girls at the school have missed large chunks of schoolwork, have dropped out, or have moved away.

Enter Boy Juma Boy, the district's Member of Parliament. He offers to pay 140 thousand shillings (a lot) to bring in the best witch doctor in the world. Which he does. There has been a lot of excitement around here because of it. Mwanamisi's husband, Mausud, is the one who contacted the MP for a cure. As he put it, "If it is a real curse, we need a witch doctor. If it is not real, we still need one because the people here all believe we need one." Our neighbor on the left is the prime suspect—a grumpy old man and quite possibly an evil wizard.

I've been talking to people about what will be done with the witches or wizards once they find them. Some say they will be forced to lick a red-hot, charmed metal instrument that won't hurt them if they're innocent. Some say they will have to eat a poisoned papaya that won't make them sick if they're innocent. Still others say they'll have to go to the District Commissioner's Office and pay a fine. Mwanamisi says people are angry enough that they might lynch the person responsible for the curse. She also said not to worry, that she and her husband would protect us from any "trouble." We are living in Salem.

Last weekend in front of crowds of maybe 1,000 villagers from around here, dressed in their most colorful *kangas,* the witch doctor arrived, dressed in capes and beads and a secondhand Lakers tee shirt. He proceeded to throw eggs into, paint chicken blood on, search for charms in, climb on the roof of, and sprinkle red holy water on three houses in a row— Mwanamisi's, the old man's, and ours. He claimed to have seen the evil spirit on the roof, in the thatching of the old man's house, but then it apparently changed into a ratlike, snakelike creature and leapt into the thatching of our house. So everyone ran over to our house while the witch doctor went inside to search for it. He even searched inside our *choo*. He found some beaded charms and other evil wizard fetishes in the other houses but not ours. Luckily.

In part, it was exciting. Everyone around us was excited too—there was dancing and singing and costumes and an exorcism to watch. To us nonbelievers, though, it was also like watching a play. The witch doctor would roll around with the invisible thing, and point in the direction it fled, describing the shapes it took as he mixed up the next concoction. The people around us would say things like "Yes, I felt the hot wind as the evil passed through me!" or "I saw it penetrate that corner of the house!" As we talked to our neighbors in the crowd, they would all start off the conversation as though they didn't believe in it, but when we reserved judgment, they would explain that it was all true, a real spirit needed to be cast out.

Then, when the whole crowd turned on our house, I felt something else. Suddenly I realized how much I didn't know about the people in the crowd. Our neighbors loved us, right? They knew we loved them, right? They wouldn't find a stray hair ball and think it was an evil charm, right? What exactly had Mwanamisi said about lynching? As I was looking at Dave and he was looking at me, Zaina, an amazing little girl, ran over to me and held my hand. Suddenly, we were surrounded by smiling neighbors. Mwanamisi told us later that they had all been worried that the evil thing had come to nest in our house, not that it had originated there. They had wanted to reassure us. (So there is nothing for you to retroactively worry about.)

Then the witch doctor cleansed our house and moved on to cleanse Mwanamisi's. He's currently narrowing down the list of suspects to a small ring of wizards who'll be punished to free the girls of the curse. People agree that it's probably the old man and his friends, and that he cursed the school because it was built on his land without his permission. It makes it all even more complicated to think that the old man might well have consulted another witch doctor and bought a curse to be placed on the school. David is visiting with Mausud now, asking all sorts of questions.

The witch doctor is on his way back, and I must go. I can tell he's coming because I just heard the animal horn he blows.

> *Gotta run,*
> *Love again,*
> *Katie*

Dear Kate,

All night long I had crank collect calls from some jail in
Virginia coming in on auto redial. The electronic voice would
say, "You have a collect call from—" and then instead of his
name some guy was saying, "I didn't do it. I didn't do it." Then
my friend Trajal gave a dance performance at 6:30 this
morning. Why so early? He wanted to "disrupt" our ideas of
how performance time fits into our lives. This was all fine and
good, but I had to get up at 5:30 and now my eyes are burning.
Is that what he wanted us to take away from his work, I want to
know.

I'm a little sad to be working again. Yes, I realize I have not
told you a thing about what I do at my new job yet. Well, it has
begun, and I'm a hundred percent relieved to have escaped the
commute to Westchester. Not only do I walk to work but the
website has a small staff, so I'm nearly meeting-free. And I'm in
a leadership position, so we'll get to see what I'm like as a boss.
My brother thinks I'll be a natural.

I was out with my former colleague Sam. He was telling me
how he had lunch with this gay guy from his office, and that
they went for sushi and he told Sam that sushi is a good
substitute for sex. This made Sam uncomfortable. He thought it
was flirty—that the implication was that they were eating sushi

because they wanted to have sex with each other. Sam said that he wanted to say, "You know, I'm not gay." I told Sam that it sounds like he's a little homophobic. He conceded, yes. I suggested that he just do what he would do with a woman— mention his girlfriend. But he hates that (as do I). Finally I told Sam that when his friend said sushi was a good substitution for sex, Sam should have said, "There's nothing like pussy." Sam had never heard me say the word *pussy*. I can't believe I just wrote that word here at work. Twice. I'd better print, send and delete this document before the corporate spies track me down, fire me for being a dirty girl, and jail me so all I can do is make crank calls.

One person who is exploring the "nothing like pussy" theory these days is Delia. Has she written to tell you that she has a girlfriend? If she hasn't already, she will, as she loves to talk about it. That's right, our Delia is dating a woman. (And I worried about her dating Stack!) Jessica is a head turner. She's very tall with dark skin and light eyes. She's only twenty-one but she's mature. Delia's very cute about the whole thing. In what may be seen as a related move, Delia has dyed over her white-blond hair to revert to her natural brown. At the same time, she has renounced the red dresses and pink frills of her blond wardrobe. Looks like somebody's search for identity is stabilizing. Needless to say, I'm glad for her. I don't think I've watched any of my friends go through this kind of transition, but, as she and I have discussed, it's no real adjustment for me. I'm mostly curious. For instance, Delia told me that she's "having a little trouble jumping the next sexual hurdle. . . ." I said, "You mean you don't want to get fancy with her stuff?" Yup, she confesses, but soon I expect I'll hear how it went. When Delia called home to say that she liked a girl, her mother's response was, "Well, you know how I feel about men." What I like most about Delia's newly discovered sexual proclivity is the implication that nothing about our lives is set in stone. Today I'm a working girl in New York and you're an intrepid do-gooder. Tomorrow you could be eating pâté and wearing black tights and I'll have run away with a lion tamer. Thank God for the unknown future.

But for now I'm still dallying with William. Last time we went hiking we lay down on a rock and ate a big Rice Krispie Treat that he had brought. I said: I didn't have you pegged as a Rice Krispie Treat kind of guy, and he said: I'm not, but I suspected you were a Rice Krispie Treat kind of girl. How true. We figured out what the clouds looked like. I saw an empty duck and a full duck. He couldn't catch the last bite of Rice Krispie Treat in his mouth and kept trying. I admitted, I'm kind of good at that (years of tossing candy corn) and threw it up and caught it on the first try. He asked, Were you a trained seal in a past life?

This weekend I'm going to DC to check on my grandparents with Josh Stack. My friends are envious that I get to spend a whole weekend with him. I want to say, Hey, aren't I just as fun? Apparently not. I haven't seen Stack for a while, but I feel clearheadedly happy about spending the weekend with him.

My grandfather has been ill lately, and while he was in the hospital, he finally married Rosa. Even though we had some warning, of course, it still happened too quickly, for Steven and me at least. But now we know Rosa a little more. The fact is that she cares for him lovingly and seems to lift his spirits. And he is truly devoted to her. So even though it's painful to know that the situation would not have appealed to my grandmother, their obvious happiness wins. It just makes me sad to see it, although, in a rather gracious way, Rosa hasn't changed much in the house, beyond adding photos of her relatives. This makes it feel like my grandmother isn't being erased. My grandfather's back at home and mostly better now. Having Stack around will diffuse the situation. I know he'll be both polite and charming, and they, like the rest of humanity, will want us to be a couple. But, although we will share the high, comfortable bed in the basement, we will behave ourselves.

I'm going to pretend to go to the gym now.

XOXO,
Hilary

Dear K8,

This follows on the heels of the package I sent you this morning.
At the post office I only had ten dollars because my bank card
went haywire, so I had to befriend the woman weighing the
package in order to get her to let me remove candy, piece by
piece, until I could afford to send it. So I babbled, "Candy for
my friend in Africa. Last time I sent her a package with
different stuff in it I could tell she liked the candy best . . ." et
cetera. So we got your package weighed and sent. Then the
postal woman said to her co-worker, "Susanna, we need to get
some candy for our jar." I was leaving with all the extra candy
when I turned at the door, went back, and handed the woman
the bag of candy pumpkins and Reese's cups saying, "For the
jar." She laughed and accepted. New York can be a small town.

Things are no longer so dreamy with William, I regret to
report. He has informed me that "something is missing." What
that means, although he made a valiant attempt to explain,
doesn't really matter. It has no point, of course, beyond the fact
that this won't work for him. Something about how he only
feels passionately about people who are unavailable. Blah, blah,
blah.

Where did this news leave us? Well, he suggested ordering
food and playing Scrabble. I said, "Scrabble won't alleviate this

news . . . but it almost will." As I leaned over to help him come up with a seven-letter word, he ran his hand down my spine and suddenly we were back in it. He tore my clothes and broke my bed and left his socks. I suspect we'll eke a few more hikes out of this experiment before it goes belly-up. Still, I've given up on this one. Even though I wasn't looking for a perfect match, I can't envision ever recovering from his statement. I'm not really surprised that this one is as doomed as the rest. Love doesn't happen to me. I'm the 7UP of romance, never had it, never will.

Oddly, the new me, amidst this ambiguity, cries easily. I was over at Stack's plying him for comfort food and watching TV for the first time since I moved to my TV-free home. We saw the news, and there was a woman who'd been blind for twelve years until her son was killed in a car accident and they gave her his corneas or retinas or something. So now she can see, and for the TV cameras they show her a picture of her dead kid and she says, "Michael (for that was his name), you said you'd always be my eyes." I cried. Then we watched *A Chorus Line,* to which my response was more in character: I fell asleep.

As if the William episode weren't my share of relationship talks for the week. Yesterday one of the producers who reports to me said that she was "sad" about a project that we're working on together—the much-needed redesign of the site—so we went outside to talk about it. I walked us toward my roof, a not bad place to talk, and she started to tell me that she has some trouble working with me in a team. (She has hit me with issues like this since I started working here. For example, out of the blue she once said, "Forgive me if I've ever been catty to you." I had no idea what she was talking about.) So she's commenting on how we've been working and it's getting confusing and I'm thinking, But there's nothing complicated here. I just want to get some work done. Yes, I am managing several people and I've never been a boss before, but I have such simple goals in this job: to make this website better and to create a pleasant working environment for all involved. I tried very hard to listen and explain, but it got us nowhere because she concluded that she wants to keep working exactly as we have been! What did she need? Assurance that I didn't consider her inferior? To express that she doesn't have the time or ability to do the job she'd like to do on this? Actually, I was pretty shocked by the whole thing. You know I pride myself on fairness. I could not understand her complaints, even though she was speaking English. Who knows? I tried. Don't you think I tried?

Also, I had a strained family dinner last night, wherein Steven, my dad and I talked about the fact that my grandfather gave some of my grandmother's jewelry to Genevieve when she and my father were still together. I find myself sentimental about everything that was my grandmother's, and I know that she expected me to have her jewelry since she said so to my mother more than once. This seems especially important now that my grandfather is remarried and I don't know what will happen with my grandmother's scarves and gloves, her clothes and books. Steven is dismayed that this could happen in the first place. He wishes our family had a stronger notion of legacy. And me, I missed my grandmother and cried at the table in the restaurant. (I was the only girl and someone had to do it.) There is no resolution, although I will eventually talk to Genevieve, with whom I am friendly, and will ask her to leave the jewelry to me and Steven or our kids.

I know it's supposed to be good to talk things over. But you know what? I'm tired of it. I say: Less talk, more Scrabble.

—H

Dear Hilary,

I can't stand the fact that I'm writing another stinking letter. I mean, it's nothing personal, I'm happy to be in mental communion with you and my family and everyone, but, geez, you know? What can I say and how can I say it—it wears me so. It's not even aesthetically pleasing since I've only got this half inkless ballpoint pen and ripped out exercise book paper. (It's always nice to complain about something the people around you are working their fingers to the bone to get, like pens, paper, and schooling so their children can learn to write.) Sigh, I can't even complain happily.

Oh, and thanks for the package! Right after I opened it I threw up. Well, not until after I had eaten all the peanut butter M&M's. Which I guess wasn't really their fault (although I was a mite suspicious of the *blue* ones!?) since I'd been sick and throwing up all week anyway. Truth be told, I actually sort of knew that I'd be throwing them up in a moment or two and really did not care. (I even admit to the fleeting thought that if I heaved quickly enough, I'd get to taste them twice, which did not actually happen.) So I just ate them down and enjoyed every morsel. I tossed Dave the Skittles to keep him away from the real game. Typically, he even has some left today. He very much enjoyed the fact that I chowed down all my candy and then yakked. A few cracks about me being a real joy on Halloween or something. Whatever. We know how to get a sugar high he's never gonna feel, right? Anyway, thanks for the treats. May all your packages return to you (different ones) a hundredfold someday like a chain letter.

After having cleaned up, or rather wiped off (cleaning up being rather an exaggeration around here), I promptly put on the new shirt you sent. Dave insisted on breathing in the aroma of American laundry detergent first. It is definitely the cleanest thing in our house. Maybe in the whole village. I looked through the photographs and thought they were of some of your new friends that I have yet to meet. Then Dave pointed out that they included shots of me. (Does it mean something that I didn't recognize myself?) So thanks for those too.

Let me interrupt this barrage of appreciation by asking if you can believe I got my butt kicked by Kenya again? I mean, my God! I was so sick with this one that at one point Dave was spooning broth into my mouth and dousing my head with the coldest water he could find like I was Mary from *Little House on the Freaking Prairie* or something. He wanted to try to get to Mombasa, but it was really late, and we probably would've had to wait forever for a vehicle. Plus, I wasn't too excited about taking the hour-long walk to get to the road. But, hey—what's a little more brain damage anyway?

Walking to school this morning the kids passing by were saying to me, "Good morning, class." And there were some one-day-old baby chicks pecking around the cassava garden.

The pineapples are growing. The old woman washing dishes in the stream said, "*Jambo*, Mama," which is a nice, kind greeting (as opposed to her previous snide mimicry of my bad accent). There was also a flattened, gray chameleon on the path next to some huge pink blossoms. Typical morning.

A little while ago, Mwanamisi's six-year-old son, Sefu, came knocking at the door to show me the decomposing bat he'd been playing with. ("Look at my bird!") The truth is that when he came to the door to show me, I looked at it, confirmed to myself that it was actually what I thought it was, and kind of smiled at him as if to say, "Yes, honey, that's a really nice rotting bat." Then Dave looked up from reading a book my uncle sent and asked, "What was that?" Only when I said, "Oh, Sefu just wanted to show me the putrid, rotting bat he was playing with," did I realize I probably could have gotten it away from him and given him a piece of chalk or something. It's shocking what no longer shocks me.

My kindhearted Indian woman neighbor Amina, who last week fed us goat knees, heard that I was sick and brought over a bottle of orange Fanta. All wrapped up in newspaper. It made me feel better even before I drank it. And Mwanamisi's youngest son, Rama, drew me a picture of a goat on the back of a flour sack. That too made me feel better. As did your package.

Delia wrote me about her new love, and I told her how very happy I am for her. Does her lover bring out the best in her?

And you. And William. Hilary, I don't think you should sleep with anyone who fails to recognize your ultimate intelligence, charisma, and sexiness. Even if he has a very good (or bad-but-compelling) reason. Just *don't* do that. It's bad for you. You're putting yourself down really subtly. Isn't he having his cake and eating it too? Let his libido force him to cut the shit. Aren't I right? I am, you know it.

(Do you feel bad for how sick I am?) (Try harder.)

Love and thanks,
K8

P.S. The witch doctor named the ring of evil wizards, including our old man neighbor, last week, but violence was averted by the fact that they had all left town already. Interesting fact: the girls are no longer having any fits.

Dear Kate,

Please please please stop being sick. Thank you.

I haven't been to many weddings. Your City Hall affair with
me as Star Witness was momentous, romantic, and did the
trick, but you have to admit that it was more of a marriage than
a full-out wedding. Well, last weekend Steven and Emily got
hitched in Millbrook, New York. There was a rehearsal dinner
in a winery that used to be an old dairy barn. We were above
where they make the wine in a huge loft space shaped like half
a barrel with a view of the sun setting over the vineyard. I made
a toast that began, "It has been brought to my attention that the
way one treats one's siblings is indicative of the way one will
treat one's spouse. So, Emily, I just wanted to let you know
what you're in for." This starter was actually a gift from Dr.
Strong, who is still making cameos.

The wedding was the next day at Emily's family's place,
down the road from the winery. It was a clear, unseasonably
cold day, and they said their vows in front of a sparkling lake.
The trees around the lake were in autumnal splendor, doubled
by the reflection in the water. Now that's peak foliage. Friends
read poems by relevant writers, including this weird poem,
which I love and have enclosed. It will remind you that even

though Emily and Steven had a much more traditional wedding than yours, they're not boring. At the last minute Emily flung two boxes into my hand and asked me to be the ring bearer. I wore a sexy, sequiny dress, so when I handed Steven the ring he said, "Thank you, Vanna." They stood arm in arm through the ceremony, practically the same height, with matching dark brown hair (though Emily has much more), and both with such open, even features. It all made sense. Emily looked like a fairy princess, Steven looked heroic, and they both cried.

I couldn't help thinking about what kind of wedding I would want to have—how there would be candy covering the whole cake, and how it might be funny and serious. Then I remembered that I don't care about being married or having a ceremony at all, although it would be a shame to miss out on a chance to be the center of attention.

I milled around at the reception able to make no conversation beyond exclaiming, "This is the happiest day of my life!" Which it was, although every time I said it I was aware that it made me sound a spinster sister. So I modified to "This is the happiest day of my life (so far)!" Before the ceremony I was helping Emily get dressed and running around doing little errands. My father was talking to the guests, and I said, sternly, "Your only son is getting ready to marry. Go be with him." Bossy, I know. But it seemed like a moment when you'd want your parents to be at hand. My dad seemed sort of on the periphery of the event—it was hard to tell if he felt happy for

Steven. He didn't say anything to that effect. But he was accidentally seated next to my grandmother, his ex-mother-in-law, and graciously escorted her through the buffet, telling her what each dish was. Later, when I asked him if he'd had fun, his only comment was "Yeah. I didn't meet anyone, did you?" Steven and Emily danced the first dance to a Leonard Cohen song, "The End of Love," and Steven then woke the older generation by slow-dancing with a man. There was much discussion about how hot my mother looked, and her fellow Herb won everybody over by dancing with my grandmother. Emily's twelve-year-old cousin displaced the band to play the Beatles' "In My Life" on his guitar. That's when Delia and I got teary.

And I was sad, as was Steven, that my grandfather wasn't there. Emily has such a big family that we could've used more Liftins. He and Rosa sent a telegram, which was appreciated because none of our generation had ever seen a telegram.

I sort of invited William to the wedding by saying something as welcoming as, "You can come if you want," knowing that, considering our limbo state, it was unlikely. At the wedding I knew some people were single and finding each other, but I was in such a blur of friends and family and forgetting names and learning the Texas two-step that I couldn't even consider it. I mean, you have to figure that just saying hello to 300 people has to take at least four hours. It felt like I barely had time to remember to drink champagne. Don't get me wrong. I was lonely. Not that I was sad during the event, but I was aware the whole time that for a long time I've been consoling myself, like any liberal arts graduate, with notions of love as a construct. As you know, I've called myself satisfied with boyfriends who were rentals with no option to buy. Now it turns out that I want to believe in love, in head over heels, go down with the ship, cut off my hair and sell my watch love.

At times I think this is damage done me a long time ago— that it's sick to have a six-year-old child playing "Someday My Prince Will Come" on the piano, to tell her that one day she will fall in love, that she will know it's right, that it will be forever. The problem was the passivity in all that romanticism. I was told I was a princess. (Think: trapped in a tower.) And the prince was supposed to come to me, if I was good, without my having to pick up the phone and make a fool of myself. It's enough to make a girl think all she has to do is look out the window or pick some flowers in the right sunlit crag for love to happen. But the wedding reminded me that there's still a version of romanticism that suits me. It comes in a few forms. I mean, Emily and Steven had a rocky start but came around. That makes me sustain hope in less than perfect circumstances. And then there's you and Dave, who seemed to have instant recognition of your affinity. That's what I'm really hoping for. Love at first sight; battlefield, Hallmark, oncoming train, frog prince love; I'll never wash this cheek again love, till death do us part love. That's why just as soon as I finish convincing myself that William is telling the truth about not wanting me, then I'll be off again, awaiting someone who'll rearrange the stars to spell out our names.

And with that endorsement, the newlyweds are off to Bangkok.

Youth! Vigor! Hope! Onward!

H

LOVE

He looks like a bowling pin, she looks like the ball.
All over the neighborhood, I meet them,
walking hand in hand, his stretching way down to hers.
They waddle-walk as really fat, or stupid, people do.
When I climb the stairs and pass their apartment
I see them sitting at their kitchen table.
They always leave their door open at dinnertime.
The smell of cabbage and old linoleum overpowers the hall.

His face is like a shy bell, fat and friendly at the bottom.
Her shape is shapeless with an overall impression of round.
He has a gray-flecked crew cut and an expression like a cow.
She has wispy mouse hair and cackles through rotten teeth.
I make small talk with them as they lumber up the stairs:
"You're out late," I say. "We're out late," he giggles.
"We're out late," she echoes. "It's late," he elaborates.
Poor, stupid, mismatched and ugly, they have love.

Yesterday, the Super told me that she was dead.
She had stepped out between parked cars and
got run over by a truck.
I walk up the stairs past their closed door
and picture him sitting on the padded chrome chair,
staring at the pearly Formica of the kitchen table,
his big, shy hands hanging between his knees, unheld,
and I cry.

Doug Dorph

Dear Kate,

No sooner did Steven and Emily take off, leaving me with the dreamy conviction that love was a neighbor, waiting for me to lend it a cup of sugar, than everything got funky. My real-life neighbor, turns out, is hardly looking for sugar. Not to be confused with the sweet but lead-footed woman upstairs, the newest threat to my sanity is my downstairs neighbor. Oh, the horror of last weekend. I wake up at 5:30 because Amy, my houseguest, is standing in my bedroom doorway. She has heard a voice saying, "Contact the police about 6L and 6M." I live in 6L. We think she's dreaming, but in the living room we hear the voice, which is my downstairs neighbor. He is yelling things like "Those people in 6L and 6M are pure shit," and "Someone's going to pay," and "Those people are involved in a murder." I am scared that he will shoot us through his ceiling. I put on more clothes. I get out my personal alarm. I am shaking so hard that my knees are knocking and my stomach is growling and I laugh at how I am such a classic scared person. I wonder if my hair will stand on end (it doesn't). We sit in the silence and dark for an hour, listening to him. I make Amy come sleep in my bed and everything seems less scary in the daylight, except that we both know it's not a bad dream. I have nothing further to report on this, except that I'm going to notify the co-op board and tread lightly.

Let's hope lunatics come in pairs, otherwise I'm doomed to endure the fairy-tale third. Freak of the week number two is Serge. We met at a party, and he asked for my number. That seemed so normal that even though I wasn't particularly interested, I was proud. I got to think, Yup, that's me, that's what I do. I go to parties and get asked on dates. But it was a bungled date. At work, we launched our redesign of the website that night. So I, duh, should not have made plans to go to a play with Serge. That was mistake number one. Also he lives on Ninth Street. I've already dated three people who live on Ninth Street in the past year (Jason, Nick, and Strong), and I'd sworn it off. But it was too late to cancel, so I went. After the play I had to call the office and, as it turned out, had to return to work. I didn't think it would take very long. They were just proofing at that point. When I asked Serge what he wanted to do—wait for me to finish or call it a night—he ducked his chin down into the high neck of his raincoat and mumbled, "I want to hang out with you." So he went to Barnes & Noble and to a restaurant and had dinner by himself while I went back to the office and one hour stretched into several. Finally I called him at the restaurant and said he should just come to the office and have a beer. So he did, and at midnight we finished and he came over to my apartment and we sat on the floor on pillows and drank red wine and kissed. I was exhausted and ambivalent, but I felt guilty for his having waited so nicely. At some point I was playing with his eyebrows and he asked what I was doing and I said that I was trying to make them more diabolical and then he confessed that he had plucked between them for the date. Something I didn't need to know. So I said, "Thanks for shaving the monobrow, but did you wax your back?" at which point he started to take off his shirt and I was like "*What* are you doing?" and he said, "I'm allowed to be naked if I want," and I said, "Not true," and he said, "I'm just proving that I don't have a hairy back." He was right. Not much hair. But then I stopped him and said, "Serge, think: First Date." I turned down his generous offer to "tuck me in" and sent him back to cursed Ninth Street. I wasn't particularly attracted to him. He was too delicately clean-cut and his eyes were too small. I liked feeling that way: intrigued but not personally involved. It runs counter to my recent revelation that I do believe in romance, but it takes the edge off William (with whom I'm still romping. I disagree with your contention that he shouldn't get to be with me. I want to be with him, actively. Wouldn't holding back be playing games? I thought we didn't do that). One point for Serge: he cleaned out my wineglasses before we used them, which was a good idea since I had tried to grow a plant in one of them and it was kind of crusty.

But, oh, you would not even believe what happened after that unremarkable beginning. Serge and I were supposed to go to a play on Saturday (apparently all he does for entertainment is go to plays but I suppose I could have stomached that for a while). So he called me at work and we made plans and then he said, "I left you a couple messages at home already." "Oh?" I said. "Yes," said he, "and one of them was obscene." "Really?" I said. Yes, and he wished he could take it back, but it was too late. So I got off the phone and called my machine and indeed he had left a message expressing a sexual fantasy involving the two of us. I don't shock easily—cybersex was a breeze—but suddenly I felt like a prude. After only one meeting I really don't want to hear a graphic and, worse, unsuccessfully poetic description of what he'd like to do to me. Know what I mean? Maybe someone could have pulled it off, but he wasn't the one. At all. You know me—ordinarily I might have saved his message, played it a few times, contemplated my response. Not this time. I listened to it once and immediately knew I never wanted to hear it again. I think I was something I don't get to be very often: disgusted. It was what the writer Malcolm Gladwell refers to as the Theory of Disqualifying Statements. "For every romantic possibility, no matter how robust, there exists at least one equal and opposite sentence, phrase, or word capable of extinguishing it."

I decided to act responsibly, because I could use some karma coupons. So I called him and, gently, nonjudgmentally, told him that his message made me uncomfortable and that I was canceling our date. He put up a decent defense, saying that he thought I'd be flattered that he found me sexy and that I'd appreciate his honesty and couldn't I just forget it altogether and that he'd just meant to be funny and titillating. My response was simply and firmly—Too bad, I didn't like it and I didn't want to go out with him that night. He persisted. Finally he said, "That message I left you—it was *art*." I returned, "Well, Serge, art is always a risk." There we left it, except that he's still leaving me messages, often. I probably will go out with him one last time, to prove to him that although I'm able to forgive the bad taste of his Disqualifying Statement, it doesn't negate the disqualification. The point is, Serge is out, men are weird and clearly my attempt to date someone who liked me more than I liked him totally backfired. Oh, drama.

Maybe I'll come to Kenya. Somehow I don't think there are scary neighbors and taboo-breaking dates in Kenya.

XOXO,

H

Part Four

October–December

DIRTY KWALE SCHOOL CLOSED

By NATION Correspondent

Public health authorities have closed down the Kwale High School owing to poor sanitation.

A source at the district's public health offices said a notice to close the school was issued on Tuesday after an inspection report indicated that the school was a health risk.

The official, who requested anonymity, said that earlier, students had gone on strike, citing poor sanitation conditions at the school.

"The situation was so bad that we had to take immediate action to avert a possible disease outbreak," he said.

The headmaster and the Education Officer could not comment as they were said to be out in the field.

Dear Hil,

We heard that my student Baya who had cerebral malaria and was put off by his teacher died two months ago. It's raining so hard that we have stopped classes because the noise of the water hitting the tin roofs is deafening.

This article from the national newspaper reports on what happened last week. Nothing has changed here at school, and now it looks like there might be yet another strike. Frankly, every day feels tense, like something's on the verge of happening. Today the kids refused to raise the flag or sing at assembly. At one point they all left the classrooms and sat outside, possibly in protest, but then it started raining and they came back in because they were getting wet. I usually try not to plan anything too complicated ahead of time so as to save myself a lot of stress.

The day before yesterday was yet another episode. Students, because of the same old things—corruption, abuse, lack of food and water, and the health risk generated by no bathrooms—burned the inside of the kitchen storeroom in an attempt to burn down the whole dining room. It happened in the middle of the night when I was at home, and I didn't hear a peep about it until the next day when I went with Owisso, another teacher who also lives off the compound, to the dining room for lunch. "Oh, it's closed," the teachers told us. Painfully slowly, the whole story came out. The teachers were trying to pretend it never happened. In truth, it almost feels like it didn't.

Dave and I overheard a conversation about all this striking while we were in a *matatu* going to Mombasa. One man was saying that each student got a quarter loaf of bread as food each day—how could they complain? The other man said he'd heard there were maggots in the porridge. The first man said, "Well, was it five or six maggots in every serving, or was it just one or two like you find at home?" (Not the same kind of conversation you overhear from your downstairs neighbor, but also scary, right?)

I had a very cold Coke and some greasy fries for lunch that tasted pretty good. Admit it, you've wanted to have a big pile of French fries and a cold Coke for lunch now and then, haven't you? I know you have.

Love,
Kate

Dear Sunshine,

It was not simply raining at the time. It was raining miserably, torrentially, hysterically. How much does it rain in the rainy season in Kenya? It doesn't matter, because this was definitely as much rain as there can be; a great, sad rain. Sane people didn't leave their apartments. But last Saturday William had little trouble convincing me to come hiking with him. There we were at Bear Mountain State Park, a mere hour or so from the metropolis, determined to see the fall leaves in their wettest, shiniest colors. There were groves of uniformly yellow leaves, then the ground would swoop up slightly and we'd be in a new city of Oz. I kept my hood on not so that I'd stay dry, which was impossible, but to try to keep the rain out of my eyes so I could see. As I walked ahead of him, though, I was near tears. I knew that I was there hoping he had come around, angry with him for daring to be my friend, wanting him to kiss me. At some point he said, "Do you hate me?" and I said, "Only a little."

We stopped by a lake for a while. The rain made its gray surface look like a parking lot. And then there was an empty parking lot with weeds sprouting through the cracked asphalt that we mistook for a lake. I know it sounds strange and not terribly interesting, but I insist that you keep an eye out for this phenomenon. Anyway, I asked William what he would do if, while we stood watching, a plane crashed into the lake. He said that he would send me for help and would swim out to the rescue. In spite of a tremor of indignation, the obvious suddenly dawned on me: that because he was a doctor (and probably a better swimmer) he could save lives that I couldn't. If that isn't adding existential crisis to heartache.

His car was the only car in the parking lot, because no one else in the entire state of New York looked out their windows Saturday morning and thought, Hey, what a perfect day for a hike! To my surprise, my companion thought we should slip out of our wet clothes and fog up those windows. I was happy to comply. Don't think I don't remember your opinion on this front. I reread it just last night and, weirdly, shed a few tears over it. Yes! It surprised me too! It was the part where you said that you didn't think I should be sleeping with anyone who didn't recognize my "ultimate intelligence, charisma, and sexiness." I don't know why those tears ran down my cheeks (although I wasn't making any noise or anything). Let's figure I was moved by

a. your faith in my excellence or
b. your correctness about my settling for too little or
c. the sadness of giving up something I'm enjoying or
d. a general sense of dissatisfaction and self-pity.

But if I don't overthink it, if I just say, every so often I have a fine time with a person I like and respect, then it seems like a simple, good thing. And the pain generated by the knowledge that he thinks something is missing isn't really so great as to overwhelm my enjoyment of his company.

And the dissatisfaction is like the wet clothes that must be put back on for the long ride home.

Love,

H

POLICE BATTLE RIOTING STUDENTS

By NATION Correspondent

Armed police officers yesterday fired canisters in the air and battled more than 400 students of Kwale High School who had gone on the rampage.

They were protesting the failure by the Provincial Education authorities to address problems facing the institution for the last two years.

Trouble started when the rowdy students went to the Principal, Mr. Daniel Igwo, and demanded to have an audience with District Education Officer Sheikh Badawi. The latter had promised to give his findings after being presented with a memorandum by the students two weeks ago.

A fortnight ago, the students boycotted classes after the school administration failed to address some of the grievances they had presented. However, they resumed classes after Mr. Badawi assured them their grievances would be looked into.

Yesterday, the students said they had boycotted classes due to poor sanitary conditions and a poor diet. Their spokesman argued that the sanitary conditions were so poor that they posed a health hazard.

Yesterday, Deputy Provincial Police Officer Peter Leiyan said police had been deployed to stop the students from causing further damage.

Dear Hilary,

I've started this letter several times already but they weren't right, so I burned them. Maybe reading the clipping I've enclosed is the best place for you to start. Just thinking about what I have to describe to you makes my stomach hurt or my body ache with nerves and emotion.

It started out like all the other mornings at school, with sweat along the waistband of my slip and tension from students stewing over the latest injustice. Just yesterday the principal pretended to raise the flag (the students had stolen it so he merely changed the position of the rope). Then he pretended that the student body hadn't turned their backs on him during the morning assembly. Yesterday, as on every other day, teachers all acted as though everything was fine, as though today would be no different. I had come to think that it *would* be no different, that this was the way of things here.

Then the principal called a staff meeting. I was excited— maybe we would talk about the fact that the school is still filthy; the bathrooms still don't exist; the food still has worms; there still isn't enough water; and there still aren't any books or materials. But that's not what was on the principal's mind. He was talking about ordering new chairs for the teachers—"tall chairs that prove we are teachers! Chairs with arms and with cloth on the seats." As he went on about the chairs, we all started to hear the yelling and shouting of an approaching crowd. The students were coming at us.

I know it's odd, but when I heard it, I was hopeful. Something is finally going to happen, I thought. Finally, this would show everyone that you can't lead a school this way. Then the screaming students surrounded the staff room, and immediately glass was breaking and blocks of the school's crumbling concrete were hurtling in at us. As students battered the door, we teachers scrambled behind tables and under the desks. Suddenly, the tenor of the screams I heard outside the door made me realize this was going to be violent. A chunk of concrete hit Immaculate, my fellow English teacher, on the side of the head. She fell over. As I stared at the blood on her head, we all heard gunshots. Now the mob was running away. The police were shooting into the crowd. As I stood there in shock, willing the bullets away from the children, another teacher said, "I hope the police kill those kids."

When I got home I hung clothes over the openings in the hut so I could get some privacy. So I could cry. Even when Dave got home (having gone to the school unknowingly to teach his afternoon class) I couldn't stop crying. I was crying because I had been hoping for violence, crying because they had shot at my students, crying because I couldn't stand being seen to be on the side of the teachers anymore, crying because it was impossible to imagine teaching here any longer. But then, tears are cheap. What does that mean? That I was only crying not bleeding.

All this means that we're going to leave Kenya. It's going to hurt. But not as much as it will hurt to stay in these schools. If only we could've just been teachers outside the school system, tutoring people who can't afford school, or setting up a center where students could come for extra help. But that is not an option. When Peace Corps finds out what happened in Kwale, they will probably try to pull us out of here and send us to yet another school. We know we don't have the energy or the spirit to move again. Besides, we have no reason to expect that the next school would be any different than the two we've left.

Since the riot I've been having a series of dreams where I meet good people I've known in my life that for random reasons I've lost touch with. In the dreams, although they're people I don't know too well or haven't thought of in years, I'm trying really hard to mend things or to catch up, and I'm telling them that I want to keep in contact with them all the time now. I think my psyche is clutching at the memory of the kindness of people. Even not-so-strangers like you.

I'm very sorry that he doesn't love you, Hilary. But I do.

Kate

NEW YORK CITY
November 21

Kate:

What are you doing? You are a teacher, not a
soldier. You must come back right away. I know if
you're admitting that things are bad then they must
be so, times ten. Do you have any hope for the
school or the village? Remember, there's plenty of
need for you here. Including my need for you to
be safe. Really.

Consider this to be serious peer pressure.

—*H*

Kate,

Okay, my friend, I'm not complaining. I know how lucky I am and all that. People starving, people with malaria, kids being unjustly beaten in unclean schools, whatever it is. But I'm still allowed to be sad, right? I'm still allowed to be hopeless and heartbroken, to wallow, to fret, to believe that love equals happiness, right? Enough. Last week I got round two of "we have to talk" from Dr. Strong, and now I'm down for the count. I knew it was inevitable because we have been in limbo for too long, pretending our awkwardness and nonrelationship were fine. But it was his birthday, and I hadn't planned to confront anything. I suppose he found his birthday ideal, though, masochist that he is. So I plunked myself down in my chair, feeling sort of like I was in a bad movie. He asked, "Don't you want to sit here?" indicating the place next to him on the love seat (oh, how ironic). I replied, "Is that your way of asking me to sit next to you?" Yes, it was. Then I got the whole recitation about how he thinks I'm great, and how it's still that he feels like there's something missing, etc. I, plea-bargaining, said, Well, we aren't getting married or anything, so if you like me and are attracted to me, as you claim to be, then why can't we just do what we've been doing? And here's where the birthday came in, I think. It seems that when you've just turned thirty-six, even though you kiss better, you're pretty marriage-focused. It wasn't worth debating. But, as he hugged me for about ten minutes, I couldn't help saying, "You're making a mistake." I just felt so sure that ending it was wrong. Not in an I-can't-live-without-you kind of way. I was totally convinced in the way that one knows if something is morally right or wrong. The decision to stop felt entirely premature, like I was still peeling the carrots and he was like, I hate this salad.

Then, to prove that this news hadn't converted me from the ideal would-be soul mate that I am, I gave him his birthday present. I had wrapped it in newspaper and then a layer of tissue. On the tissue paper I drew a circle around some of the words that showed through from the newspaper: "Fire will prevail." Inside were thirty-six candles and a set of twelve matchboxes from Chinatown, each of which says something like "Achievement," or "Money," or "Love" and has a fortune in it. We tried to name all the colors of the candles, usually resorting to fruits and vegetables (eggplant, kiwi, okra). He was making regular, see-we-can-be-friends conversation, and I was trying to cry. I know you're thinking, How unlike Hilary. But I wanted to, because there was little else to say, because I wanted to prove to us both that this was real and final. I told him that I couldn't be friends with him and that I didn't want him to call me. At that, he looked so sad that again I felt like I was watching the same bad movie, scene two. Finally, when he hugged me goodbye at my door, I managed to sob into his overcoat. And then I felt a little proud of myself, somewhere in the unhappiness, for knowing exactly what I wanted.

I realize how this may sound in context of the crisis in Kwale, but love counts, even in wartime.

Hilary

Dear Hilary,

I have no hope for the school. It has never reopened after the
stoning. It's closed for the rest of the year but not for cleaning
or repairs or to dig *choos* or to find a way to supply the place
with water—it's closed as punishment to the boys, so they'll
miss school time and fail the all-important National Exam. The
headmaster left, but not because he was forced out of office for
flagrant abuses of power. No, rumor has it he got a promotion
to a more prestigious school. While the school has been closed,
teachers have been meeting to discuss the Readmission
Procedures for the boys.

After the first strike, several months ago, the Readmission
Procedures were that each boy had to submit to an
interrogation, and had to sign a Confession of Guilt (many
innocents were forced to sign it) and an Oath of Obedience to
the school authorities. Then, he had to lie facedown in the dirt
while a teacher beat him with a thick rod. For the teachers to
do this to each of the 400 boys took more than a week of
teachers bellowing, the cane whipping through the air, and
students screaming in pain and humiliation. The assistant
headmaster even asked that I take my turn at the interrogation
tables and at the cane (although he knew that I wouldn't). I left
so I wouldn't have to listen to the cries.

Now the teachers have decided that the reason for the stoning riot was that those procedures were too lenient. The meetings are spent devising harsher measures. Needless to say, I am no longer attending the meetings. I have no hope that the school will ever be any different than it is now.

Do I have hope for the village? Well, hope for what? I have no hope that the children will, in the foreseeable future, be as healthy, or have as many choices in their lives as American children. I mean, I got out of bed at 5:30 this morning to burn garbage and dump compost because I'm not brave enough any other time. It's embarrassing for everyone when the children try to save the rotting food we throw away. Last time Dave sneaked out to do it when he thought no one was looking, little Mwanaidi spied him and ran over with a few of her friends to eat the compost. Dave was fishing for the Kiswahili word for "putrid" but settled for "very bad." He coaxed her into dropping it. Worse yet, as our trash heap was burning they began trying to fish out of it a pair of underwear I had used to tend to some impetigo, the pair now covered with pus, blood, and bacteria I had scraped off my face. (I used the underwear because it was clean and semidry. No towel will ever reach that state.) Luckily, Dave came back in time to catch them before they ran off with that contagious prize. (This morning it was just me and the chickens. I was curious to see if they are dumb enough to actually walk into a flaming pyre to get banana peels, and yes, they are.)

Actually, I would have great hope for Kenya's future if three-year-old Uba were going to be president someday. Yesterday she wandered over here while I was peeling potatoes. She's about two feet tall, sucks her fingers, talks a lot, and has a tendency to find your lap no matter what position you are in. She got excited watching me peel, rushing to get a pot from the far side of the courtyard, filling it with water, and dragging my *jiko* (container for my cooking fire) out from under the thatching. We weren't quite ready to eat, so Dave and I were just chatting with her brother Rama. The next thing I knew, Uba had loaded the *jiko* with charcoal, gathered dried palm leaves for kindling, and was searching the kitchen for matches. Playing along, I took the lighter and pretended to light the charcoal. Then I put the pot on and thanked her for helping me. She looked at me as if I were a nincompoop and took the pot off the nonfire. She got some more palm leaves, flicked the lighter, and started blowing on the tiny sparks and fanning the flame with a pot lid she'd found. She brought the potato peelings out to the chickens, washed the peeling knife, and swept the courtyard with a bundle of tied-together reeds while she was waiting for the potatoes to cook. After a little while she even tasted a piece to see if they were ready! At one point while she was getting leaves right in under the charcoal, she burned herself a little, shook her hand for a second, and kept on working as she sucked on the blister. Remember, she's three years old! What spunk! We all ate potatoes together and I thought about how we are leaving here.

Kate

Dear K8,

On Monday I was diligently following my new program of
going to the gym before work. I got into the elevator, but it
stopped on the floor below mine. I had a sinking moment of
premonition. Then the doors opened, and standing there was a
middle-aged guy—not clean, not dirty—whom I somehow
instantly identified as my downstairs neighbor who freaked me
out last month and has been yelling weird things intermittently
ever since. He said, "Do you live in 6L?" I said yes. He looked
at me in disgust and growled, "What do you think you're
doing?" Then, shaking his head, he started to walk away.
Because I know he's strange (and have gotten more information
on this front from the doormen), I figured I should try to
establish my innocence. I stepped out of the elevator and said,
"I'm not doing anything. I just want to be a good neighbor to
you." He turned and replied, "Well, I don't think sending
pulses into someone's apartment is being a good neighbor."
This confirmed something that a tenant had told me—that this
guy believes, and has for many years, that his upstairs neighbors
(currently me) are sending electrical pulses down into his
apartment. There I was, in my gym clothes, looking, I felt, very
small and harmless. I said, "I don't know what you're talking
about, but I'm not doing anything." He asked if I was "alone up

there." I affirmed that I was. Then he said, "Well, somebody's trying to kill me . . ." I was okay with that, thinking I'd successfully asserted my innocence. But then he added, ". . . and if it's not you then I think you know who it is," and turned away. I called feebly after him, "I'm really not. . . ." Then he was gone.

I waited for the elevator to come back, and this time, as luck had it, it was full of people, including a very nice member of the co-op board. I looked at him and said, "That man just *confronted* me!" and burst into tears. In fact, I cried silently the whole time I was on the Elliptical Crosstrainer at the gym because, upsetting situation or no, I needed to get my workout in. The humor of this did not escape me. I was intermittently weepy all day, freaked out at the proximity of this guy, who is separated from me by a mere layer of wood panels, and possibly some plaster. Oh how this ruins my safe, sweet nest.

Then I set about trying to figure out what could be done. I spoke to lawyers, the police, the co-op board, mental health authorities, my parents, and assorted other smart people about what I can do and what they would do if they were so lucky as to be me. Some of them were funny. Like when I went to the police I said to the guy at the front, "I'd like to file a harassment report." He said, "Who are you harassing?" I answered, "My downstairs neighbor is harassing me. He thinks I'm trying to kill him by sending electrical pulses through the floor." The policeman said, "Well, are you?" I replied, "Officer. I'm not here to confess." Similarly, when I spoke to the National

Alliance for the Mentally Ill and explained what was going on the guy said, "Well—why don't you stop sending the pulses down there?" Later he suggested that turning up the voltage might help. Everyone's a comedian, and all I can say is, Take my downstairs neighbor, please!

For now, it's unsolvable. Practical, sane, and assertive I may be (and we can debate that another time), but there appears to be no instant solution to this problem. Not only is it insane but it's unfair. I'm quiet, and I help out my elderly neighbor, Esther. I hold the door-open button for others. I recycle. I keep to myself. I try to be good. I envy your ability to escape by coming home. I'm keeping in mind how relieved you will be to have certain amenities, all of which I already enjoy. I'm also considering, you know, others less fortunate. Compared with you, Kwale villagers, and plenty of U.S. citizens, my situation is not bad. But compared to me, it sucks. Every day in the paper there's somebody who gets murdered by that weirdo down the hall. It's so easy to envision the people I talk to now going around saying, "Oh my God, she was just telling me about this guy last week. She knew he was nuts. There was nothing she could do and now she's dead."

I'll tell you, right now for the first time ever I wish I had an overprotective father who couldn't stand to have his daughter in a potentially dangerous situation. Or, and this in light of recent events, I wish I had a fellow, wimpy or no, who would wake up at night when I hear this guy raving. As you would testify, company makes all the difference. Right now, I'm pretty alone.

However, one of my doormen offered to "teach that guy a lesson," which was so sweet it almost made me cry again. And a burly friend at work who used to be a bouncer offered to pay the guy a visit and shut him up. Stack came over and helped me finish a bottle of wine on a night when Freako was yelling, "You're the guilty one" and "You murdering cocksucker. You have no right to live in an apartment" and other lunacies at top volume. These gestures stand out, and I appreciate them, but what I would give for the constancy of a companion. A big dog, maybe? Maybe now's the time to indulge my desire for a weimaraner named Focus. Somehow this situation demands more than a cat.

I'm probably not in immediate danger (although the doctor I spoke to at Bellevue said that I was). I do feel safe behind my doors, and I now have a fireman's key to the elevator so I run express down to the lobby. But this really has soured my dreamy apartment. So much for independence. So much for privacy. I've always taken off my shoes to walk around, as you know, but now I get a palpable wave of anxiety when a guest drops something.

Luckily, work, as the cliché goes, is something of an escape from my troubles at home. You would not believe some of what I do: look at the best ways for data to be shown; FTP files to the stager, that kind of thing. I barely use the phone now. Why talk when you can email? I still feel like I'm out of my field, since I work on computers without even owning a television. But maybe that's what it feels like for a lot of people. Not forest rangers, but people who own tissue factories don't necessarily have hay fever, do they?

Love,
H

Dear Hilary,

There are eight munchkins gathered at the window nearest to
where I am writing. They are contorted into pretzel-like shapes
in order to watch me. I tried sitting on the porch, but there
they lost interest and were just pestering me for tin cans.
Peering in the window is much more fun. Then they can
knock each other over getting the best view. You'd think they'd
get bored since they've watched me a million times before, and
I'm not wiggling my ears or anything.

We have a development in the "our house" front. Actually,
not a development, more like a roommate. Our landlord has
moved back here. Right here. It's particularly crowded because
he has a lot of relatives who come and go freely, and the house
is not large to begin with. This eliminates any shred of privacy
left to us. He's quite polite, but since he's an *mzee* (old person)
and the landlord, he has the Kenyan right to boss us around.
Especially me (I'm a girl). I don't like it. It makes clear that the
goodness we're leaving behind in Kenya—the people in this
village—we would have had to leave anyway, even if Peace
Corps didn't make us, since we'd go crazy living with this guy.
Although not as crazy as I'd go living above your guy. Are you
okay? I miss you. I'm not going to talk about it.

Kate

Dear Kate,

I've been better, I don't mind saying. The last trickle of William
is that he left me a bag of guilt gifts, including a fortune cookie.
I broke it open and there was the fortune "Fire will prevail." It
took me a stunned minute to realize he must have had it
custom-made to say what I'd said on his birthday gift. Also,
folded up into a tiny scrap at the bottom of the bag, as if it
were a wish that didn't need to be found, was a prescription,
written on his prescription pad, for "eternal happiness." Every
few nights Delia helps me fight the urge to call him. I ring her
up with some brilliant conversation starter like, "Hey. It's me.
I'm not calling William, right?"

"Right," says Delia.

"Right," I say. "Um, why, again?"

I hate the idea that he continues to pay his phone bills, to
button his shirts, to age, to eat, to read or not read the
newspaper. I hate that he lives in real time, that everything he
does involves the decision that he didn't want to do it with me.
Somewhere he's filling up his gas tank and I'm thinking about
how I'd like to see the way his arm looks doing that. I'm
thinking about how he held his coffee cup when he drove.
How his fingers looked, by themselves and against mine. How
his sentences came slowly, for reasons I won't find out. How

tired he was, how sad and tired all the time and determined to
be well and good. How I wanted to heal him, not by helping
him or carrying him but by huddling next to him. How I
wanted to have his whole world, to move it in some way across
my body, or to digest it, to have it be at once foreign and part of
me. I wanted him to talk forever for the sound of his voice, for
what he said and what made him think of it and what it made
him think next, for how it sounded in the trees or in a room,
for what the room said back.

I keep locking myself out of my apartment. I have yet to
descend into listening to Tom Waits on repeat, but I feel
hollow. Is that a cliché? Well, good for it. I'm drowning in
sorrow and you're giving me a hard time? I want to be a hermit
in a cave with a sunny ledge and a pet flower. This isn't a
breakup, Kate, this is a breakdown of what is right and good in
the world. It has done something devastating to all that I am.

Now, Kate, will you hurry up and come home. Hurry and
tell me this isn't my life.

—H

Dear Exile,

Everyone is awakening. I can hear mamas sweeping the ground
with stick bundles, roosters crowing, the radio with its ever-
present theme song, and an occasional mother yelling, *"Wey!"*
(short for *wewe,* as in "You, get over here!"). In a little while I'll
search down the matches and boil some water for tea. Then I'll
buy some fried *mandazi* from Nazmin, who sits with a bucket
of them in front of the *duka.* She'll wrap them in newspaper,
and I'll wake up Dave for breakfast. All this makes me a little
sad. Soon, I'll be gone. When we got home from shopping
yesterday, about twenty neighborhood kids were singing and
dancing an African dance on our porch. They ran toward us,
giggling and welcoming us home, probably for the last time.

All this sadness creeps up only now because we've been busy
with a flurry of loving goodbye rituals. As we give all our things
away and have last visits, kids are giving us drawings they made
with our markers, their mothers slaughter chickens or sew for
us, and the men stop by for man-chats. It almost makes me
doubt our decision. But then I remember school, and I know
that we will certainly go.

Zaina (she's the one who held my hand during the exorcism)
and two of her friends just came over, wearing blue sateen
party dresses covered by ripped *kangas,* to find out what time

we are leaving tomorrow and to play cards. We played a game
that they usually play without me because I'd never understood
the rules to it. I had always thought it was something like hearts,
since after everyone put a card in the middle, someone took the
trick, but I could never figure out which card to play and could
never figure out who would take the trick. For some reason, I
never succeeded in understanding their explanations of how it
was played either. As I tried to play today, it suddenly hit me—
they weren't using *any* rules, they were just playing with the
cards in a gamelike way. It was fitting that for the last game I
could join right in. Zaina gave me the brightest smile ever, and
giggled, covering her teeth the way she always does.

I hope you still love me when I come home all twisted up.

Yours come Christmas,
Kate

Dear K8,

I escaped this weekend to my dad's place in Connecticut, bringing, for support, Steven and Emily and Stack. Stack and I took a nature walk and I depetaled a daisy, reciting, "He loves me. He loves me not . . ." When the last petal was He loves me not, I changed the rules to include the daisy's yellow center. I popped it off and tossed it up victoriously: "He loves me!"

At a slow, candlelit, family-style dinner, Emily had a few drinks and I got her to publicly admit that her marriage to my brother was merely a fringe benefit of her friendship with me. We slept in two adjoining rooms, and Stack and I had to tell Emily and Steven that we could hear everything and to give them a firm "no hanky-panky" rule. The best part was that at six in the morning up on the roof there sprang such a clatter that it woke everyone up. It's otherwise completely silent countryside out there, and I think we were all staying silently in bed trying to figure out what the very loud, repetitive, awakening noise might be. I got out of bed and stared at the ceiling for a while, and then left the room. The place is a big, open barn, so from where I stood I saw down into the living room, where a bright red cardinal (not the perpetrator of the noise) was fluttering at the window. I whispered to Stack (who from our earlier walk seemed more into birds than I would've guessed) that there was a cardinal, but he declined to get up. Then, far too awake, I wandered into the bathroom, from which I had a good view of the roof. On the peak, perfectly poised in the very front of the house, was the culprit. There perched a woodpecker, pecking, oblivious to the hours we keep. I went to tell Stack, and suddenly he, Steven, Emily, and I were all in the bathroom, just staring at the bird. It felt like Christmas, with the four of us up too early, gazing in awe at our rooftop visitor.

In that moment I totally forgot how sad I've been about Strong, and scared of the neighbor, and everything else. What an unexpected relief it was to be in one place at one time. Who knows how long we would have stood there watching the bird destroy the house so prettily. Soon he got stage fright and was gone. As we filed back to bed, teeth chattering, Emily walked behind me with one hand on each of my shoulders. Stack made a bad joke about Pinocchio and the woodpecker, and I thought of something Delia says when she's happy, "This is so enough."

I guess this is the last letter I will send, Kate, and, in a way, I hope it reaches you before you leave. Given the choice, however, I'd prefer that you not wait for it. I want you home, thank you. Of course, I won't cherish you so much when you're here, within reach of balanced meals and hospitals, but I'll still like you. I'll even take your calls.

Maybe when you try to get a life here you'll realize that finding an apartment in New York City is a little like squeezing a sac of spider eggs out of your foot, plus there's the broker's fee. Bring me a little something, and sleep on the plane so you can keep your eyes open when I see you. I'll call your mother for a plan; I will do whatever I am told to do. I'm glad that you will be home soon, weary one. Home in time for gingerbread cookies (if you like that kind of thing) and the lit-up trees in Central Park. How about we go to the Angelika and watch movies for a whole Saturday?

With relief,
H

Postscript

Kate came home on Saturday, December 22—just in time for Christmas. It was pouring that day, and I left early to take the long bus ride to the airport. I sat on the bus, watching all the other passengers struggle to bring on their luggage. My wallet was in my raincoat pocket, and my hands were empty on my lap. I was still a basket case over William. I kept reminding myself that Kate was coming home, the way in a scary movie I look at my hands, the other moviegoers, and the walls of the theater to remind myself that when the movie is over I will walk out into daylight. As I stared out the window, I was overwhelmed by that mixture of yearning and nostalgia that emerges on moving vehicles. The timing was strange—all I really wanted was to watch Kate and Dave eat some real food and to delight in their homecoming, to see with my own eyes that they were finally safe. But it's never really convenient to be miserable, and I felt lucky to have Kate's coming home as a distraction that was large enough to be its own event.

When they walked off the plane, the mothers and Dave's sister ran to meet them. The fathers and I held back. Kate and Dave were both bony and tired-looking, and Dave had an unexpected beard. I realized I'd been afraid that Kate would look unfamiliar, or yellow with malnutrition. She was scrawny, with an older look in her eyes, but she wasn't as sun-damaged as I was afraid she'd be. Above all, she was walking and she was Kate.

At the water fountain she cried at the sight of water so translucent and cold, so accessible. Everything—the airport, the people, the cars—looked preternaturally clean and bright to her. After all the parents promised that I wouldn't be invading family time, we drove in a caravan to Dave's family home. We knew the returned travelers were exhausted. They couldn't eat, not homemade lasagna, not ice-cream sundaes (though I did remarkably well considering my own suffering), and they couldn't really talk. Kate wanted to shower, which she did, twice. Watching them made me remember those moments of extreme exhaustion, when the idea of a bed is so deeply appealing that it overwhelms all capacity to take the necessary steps to bring oneself there.

I just observed them, taking comfort in their physical presence. And they were taking the same kind of comfort, asking practical questions, delighting in kitchen appliances and plumbing. Dave told us that when he hugged his sister the memory of layered scents rushed at him: he could smell that she used shampoo and soap and perfume and laundry detergent. We looked at photos, but the travelers were too tired to explain what we were seeing. The wood-burning stove sent a soporific warmth into the room. Kate struggled to stay awake; the air was heavy with contemplation and weariness and we were quiet.

In the middle of that night I awoke in the narrow bed of one of Dave's sisters. I was covered with several wool blankets and the window was slightly open to let in the sound of the nearby stream and the rain. I sobbed into the sound of the stream, hoping I wouldn't be heard. Kate was back, and I knew, after some sleep and food, we'd reflect on this. But she had escaped her struggle and I hadn't. We were off-balance and what would happen now? Once we lived together. Once we wrote letters. Sometimes she needed me, sometimes she sheltered me. Now she was downstairs, asleep, overwhelmed with circumstance, with few plans for tomorrow. Now I was upstairs in the same house, awake and alone in the quiet rain.

—*Hilary Liftin*

Epilogue

I'm sitting on the subway with my shoulder bag and my bagel, on the way to my new teaching job. As we calmly speed uptown, my eyes wander a little. A part of a headline jumps out from the newspaper of the man in front of me . . . RIOTING IN NAIROBI. Before I can read any more, the man gets off. Suddenly, I realize where my body is and where it isn't, and I have that funny sensation that everything in the world happens at the same time. I look around, and no one else on the subway seems to think this is strange.

Things have seemed this way ever since we've gotten back: un-strange. The hot shower works each morning, the food tastes familiar, trains come, and I generally understand both the words and the meaning when people talk to me. For the most part, I feel safe and in comfort, and I trust the people around me are not so very different. I feel lucky.

At the same time, I find myself waiting for a thunderstorm. I breathe when the rain is pouring down, defying the indoor feeling of the streets. When the light flashes and the sky crackles,

Dave and I look at each other, and think about another part of the planet.

I don't speak with Hilary much, she's rarely home. It's hard to keep in regular contact now that we live in the same city, but we manage. She continues to date and, occasionally, to pine. She continues to receive promotions, and the last time she tried to explain her new job to me, I pretended to understand. I suspect she knew I was pretending.

Several weeks ago Hilary invited me to join her and what she expected would be "a few friends" at a quirky bar in Tribeca to celebrate her birthday. I arrived and was not at all surprised to see under the smoky lights a crowd of about fifty people, many gathered around her as she told a funny story about how she has no life. She stood there in the center of the circle in a gauzy black dress and glittery blue eye shadow talking and gesticulating, at her side an enormous pile of candy—lollipops, circus peanuts, gumdrops, and candy corn—all gifts. She smiled at me as I arrived and went on with her story, and I knew that soon she would come over and just have time to point out a few of her promising suitors before she would again be swept away amidst the murmurs. I knew this was the quintessential Hilary, and she would excuse my inappropriate attire and early departure, as always. We exchanged looks twice more before I left, once when I caught her eye as she swore she would never again eat a piece of candy, and again when she, knowing of my pregnancy, smiled at me as I refused a drink.

I'd like to believe there will be a time in the not-so-distant future when we'll sit, I with my bulging belly and she in her wool suit, sipping water or coffee, eating bread or cake, and we'll have more time to talk.

—*Kate Montgomery*

Acknowledgments

Thanks to Cindy Klein Roche, who is so much more than a perfect agent; Robin Desser, who knew how to make these letters into a book; and to the people without whom this book wouldn't be the same: Sarah Burnes, Amy Capen, Semi Chellas, Susan Choi, Chris Fendrick, David Fore, Matt Love, Ben Moser, Betsey Schmidt, the people at Vintage, our always-supportive families, and the boys on the board, who know what they did.

This book is dedicated to David Hackenburg, who is Kate's everything and Hilary's something.